IMAGES
of Wales

TREORCHY
MALE CHOIR

Best wishes
Dean Powell

EISTEDDFOD MARQUEE
TALBOT PADDOCK - KINGTON
SUNDAY, 21st JUNE, 1959

Doors open, 7.30 p.m — To Commence at 8 p.m.

=== FIRST VISIT ===
Treorchy Male Voice Choir
FIRST PRIZE WINNERS
AT THE
ROYAL NATIONAL EISTEDDFOD
EBBW VALE, 1958

ALSO BROADCAST ON B.B.C. HOME
SERVICE SERIES:
— "AELWYD Y GAN" —
AND
B.B.C. LIGHT PROGRAMME SERIES
"MID-DAY MUSIC HALL."

GRAND CONCERT
BY THE
TREORCHY MALE VOICE CHOIR
(OVER 100 VOICES)

Conductor : Mr. JOHN H. DAVIES.   Accompanist : Mr. TOM JONES.

CHAIRMAN : REV. C. J. HARDING (Presteigne).

TICKETS: 7/6 - 5/- - 3/6 ===== OBTAINABLE FROM:

Mr. JAMES PROTHEROE, Hergest, Kington – Tel. 240.

Mrs. M. DAVIES, Fish & Game Shop, Church Street, Kington – Tel. 108.

or from any Member of the Committee.

Proceeds in aid of KINGTON EISTEDDFOD FUNDS

R. & E. Hopkinson, Printers, Kington.

Treorchy Male Choir Concert Poster, Talbot Paddock, Kington, Sunday 21 June 1959. In compiling this publication, the author would like to thank all those who kindly donated pictures and information. Also to Roger Morse, Alwyn Lewis and Stuart Hill for their support, friendship and assistance always. And especially to Norman Martin, Choir Registrar and Honorary Archivist since 1963. Without his exceptional contribution and guidance this publication would not have been possible.

IMAGES
of Wales

TREORCHY
MALE CHOIR

Compiled by
Dean Powell

TEMPUS

First published 2001
Copyright © Dean Powell, 2001

Tempus Publishing Limited
The Mill, Brimscombe Port,
Stroud, Gloucestershire, GL5 2QG

ISBN 0 7524 2238 3

Typesetting and origination by
Tempus Publishing Limited
Printed in Great Britain by
Midway Colour Print, Wiltshire

This publication is dedicated to the memory of Rhodri Wynne Jones (1976-2001)

Daeth a'r dydd i'r llefydd llwyd
A'r haul i lonni'r aelwyd.

Author Dean Powell (right) with good friend and fellow chorister Stuart Hill, Sydney, Australia, 1999. A graduate of the University of Wales College of Swansea where he obtained a Bachelor of Arts degree in English and Welsh, Dean is the Editor of the *Pontypridd & Llantrisant Observer* and Literary Editor of *The Western Mail*. A member of Treorchy Male Choir since the age of 16, he was Publicity Officer for eight successful years and has undertaken a series of tours to Australia, Canada and the USA as their tenor soloist as well as performing regularly in venues throughout the UK.

Contents

Foreword

Singing with the Treorchy Male Choir is the hardest thing I have ever done – because it's not easy to sing with a lump in your throat and a tear in your eye. That is the effect it has on me to be stood in front of my fellow Welshmen listening to those beautiful voices. I refer, of course, to the television shows the men of Treorchy have done with me and on those occasions the cameras and all the other things that go to make up a television studio have been lost in insignificance.

No less emotional were the impromptu concerts the choir gave us in the studio canteen afterwards. In fact, I took my father out to the studio on the second occasion, because I knew how much he would enjoy it. A wonderful experience.

There is nothing like the sound of a Welsh male choir, and the Treorchy is the finest. They have represented the best of the Welsh voice for generations with honour and integrity. They are our international ambassadors.

But it's not just that, I know the complete joy of a singer, and it is that personal, individual experience with singing that gives so much to life. It lifts everyday existence right out of the ordinary, each singer knows he's special, and he knows what he gives to the group.

The commitment of the choir properly serves the music it performs, and that is the ultimate gift.

Congratulations and all the best wishes for continued success in the future

Tom Jones, Honorary Member Treorchy Male Choir
Los Angeles, California
2001

Tom Jones receiving Honorary Membership of the Treorchy Male Choir following the recording of his Christmas show, *This is Tom Jones*, at the Borehamwood Studios, which was broadcast on Christmas Day, 1969.

Introduction

This is not just a choir, it's a way of life.

The origin of that present day phenomenon, the Welsh male choir, can be traced to the fusion of two easily discernible features of valley life in the nineteenth century – the strength of nonconformity as a religious force and the frantic acceleration of the coal mining industry. While the Rhondda was penetrated indiscriminately by those early pioneers, exploiting the mineral resources and transforming the valley floor into something of vast black Klondike, communities were galvanized by a musical intensity the like of which had never been seen before. For more than a century it was famous for more than just its outpouring of precious bituminous fuel, it was the heartland of a culture inspired by the sound of people united in music.

Like a microcosm of the 'Land of Song' itself, Rhondda was a melting pot of a whole range of musical organisations and within those monotonous terraces the universally popular image of the male voice choir first found its voice. It became a social feature for groups of men showing passionate loyalty to the villages of their birth – and adoption – to unite in song in chapel vestries, usually under the conductorship of a fellow worker, whose formal knowledge of music was often rudimentary but whose intuitive grasp of management and musical inspiration defied description. Steeped in eisteddfod rivalry and mastery of tonic solfa, combined singing inflamed passions like tribal warfare and the golden era of choralism was born.

It was from such inauspicious beginnings way back in 1883 in a hometown pub, the Treorchy Male Choir first found its voice and developed into what is probably the most famous male voice combination in the world. During the nineteenth century the original Treorky Male Choir (it really was spelt that way!) claimed two first prizes at the National Eisteddfod and gave a royal command performance for Her Majesty Queen Victoria at Windsor Castle. But despite these early successes they only mark the beginnings of what can be called a protracted gestation period as consistency in success was to elude the choir for many years.

The choir existed in many guizes for the next sixty years, but one element that remained constant was their undiminished enthusiasm. All that was needed was for someone to lead them from the relative wilderness to the elusive forefront of the Welsh choral tradition. Massive economic depression, coupled with the brunt of two world wars, took its toll on the organization and it eventually disbanded in the summer of 1943. At the end of the Second World War, with life returning to normality, a group of young men gathered with the intention of re-forming the choir. Their prayers were answered on 16 October 1946 – a date to remember in the annals of Welsh music – because John Haydn Davies, a diminutive, self taught and diffident school teacher, accepted the invitation to become the conductor of the new Treorchy Male Choir. This remarkable man, a disciplinarian and diplomat par excellence, lead them to a 'realm of gold' in the space of twenty years, transforming the raw music recruits into an internationally renowned choir who possessed something new in Welsh music – a controlled, and distinguishable sound.

They scaled the peaks of musical distinction in the eisteddfod field by gaining a record eight national wins, making a total of twenty-two 'firsts' out of twenty-seven entries. The 'Treorchy Sound' was heard worldwide as they made regular radio broadcasts, television appearances, commercial recordings and two feature films. In 1963 the choristers undertook their first overseas tour to Switzerland and were honoured in being the first Welsh choir to perform in the Royal Concert of St Cecilia in the presence of Her Majesty the Queen.

When ill health took its toll on John Haydn Davies, John Cynan Jones was invited to join the choir as associate conductor and there followed three happy years of music making together. During this time the choir made its last appearance in the competitive arena and in January 1969 John Haydn felt the time had come to finally hand over the reins to his heir apparent and announced his retirement. The legacy was accepted with respect and pride. Remembering the idiom that 'change is the only constant thing in life', it was obvious from the choir's repertoire that John Cynan possessed the breadth of vision to take them into new dimensions of musical experience.

Treorchy became the first male choir to venture into the uncharted territory of popular music and collaborations in television shows with celebrities such as Ella Fitzgerald, Julie Andrews, Burt Bacharach, Tom Jones, and Sir Harry Secombe convinced them of the value of this 'new talent'. It led to what was nothing short of a revolution in the format and content of concert programmes because what had been considered almost outlandish in musical terms was suddenly acceptable. Alongside the works of Grieg, Wagner and Verdi appeared Andrew Lloyd-Webber, Stephen Sondheim, Paul Anka and John Lennon. Subsequently the choir has made almost fifty commercial recordings, making it the most recorded in the UK, and arguably, the world.

During the 1980s the choir undertook an enviable number of overseas tours, including two visits to Canada, a performance in Strasbourg Cathedral for its congregation of nearly 4,000 people and became the first Welsh choir to perform in the Sydney Opera House. It was a matter of weeks before the choir's tour of the Mid-West States of America in 1991 when the worst possible scenario took place – they were forced reluctantly to accept John Cynan's premature resignation. He was replaced by John Jenkins, a man of immense musicality and born leadership, who led them on their first successful US tour, entertaining capacity audiences in Nebraska, Minnesota, Iowa and Washington D.C.

Following in the footsteps of his predecessors, John was eager to develop the choir's enormous repertoire and to this end Treorchy became the first choir, outside Finland, to perform Sibelius' *Kullervo Symphony* in its native tongue. In the never-ending quest to maintain choral traditions but to be progressive in the modern idiom, the choir went on to release a rock album of music by Queen. During his six years as musical director John Jenkins led the choir on two further US tours which included Georgia, California and Colorado.

History was to repeat itself when a previous deputy conductor, Andrew Badham, became the choir's fourth musical director, leading them on to greater glory with a legendary sell out, month-long tour of Australia and further visits to Canada and the United States, again for capacity audiences. Andrew's immense musicality and visionary perspective is already heralding a bright future for our much-loved choir.

Within these covers, you are allowed just a mere glimpse, or rather the tip of the proverbial iceberg of what is more than just a choir, but a way of life. To tell the full Treorchy story would take volumes, capturing the spirit of a camaraderie of colourful characters who are devoted to ensuring their high standards of musical excellence are maintained for generations to appreciate. This publication will praise the vision of the founder members, the often under-valued virtues of loyalty and dedication which imbued so many choristers, the strength of will and collective determination of successive officers, commitment and the artistic purpose which was inspired by every conductor and accompanist. In modesty, the past is one of fulfilment. The future must be one of optimism and quiet confidence. Great deeds have been done and exciting times lie ahead.

The Treorchy Male Choir is bound together and united in the common purpose of the enjoyment of music making and of giving pleasure to others. We look forward to upholding our fine reputation as we lead the Welsh choral tradition forward into the new millennium.

Dean Powell
Tŷ Ffynnon
Llantrisant
April 2001

One
Myfanwy
1883-1943

What wonderful voices they have.

Her Majesty Queen Victoria

Treorky Male Choir, 1895. A group of twenty-five singers won the first prize of £1 in an eisteddfod at the Red Cow Hotel in the summer of 1883 for their performance of *Myfanwy*. Aged between eighteen and twenty-two, they were members of Treorchy United Mixed Choir, who gathered to practice for a farewell concert for a fellow chorister. They proved so successful that they became a fresh entity under the direction of George Thomas 'Bach'. Open air rehearsals were held at Stag Square and Cardiff Arms Square, before moving into the Treorky Hotel.

William Thomas, conductor, Treorky Male Choir, 1885-1896. Born in Mountain Ash in 1851, he conducted his grandfather's winning choir in an eisteddfod at the age of ten. He came to Treorky in 1873 as choirmaster of Noddfa Baptist Church, School's Attendance Officer for Ystradyfodwg and manager of the Treorchy Co-operative Store. A strict teetotaller, he only accepted the invitation to conduct the Treorky Male Choir if they left the Treorky Hotel and moved to the nearby school, resulting in a drop in membership because of the lack of liquid refreshment! Under his baton the choir achieved national acclaim.

Treorky Male Choir founder members John Rees, Phillip Watkins, William Thomas (Bosh), Jacob Davies, Thomas Bebb, John George, James Evans, David Walters, Eben Evans, Sam Rees and Edward Rees, 1883. Conductor Griffith Rhys Jones 'Caradog', landlord of the Treorky Hotel, formed his own male voice choir in 1871, but it was William Thomas who put the town firmly on the musical map. In the autumn of 1883 they won 30s in an eisteddfod at the Corner House Hotel with David Miles, checkweigher, and Timothy Davies, postmaster, as adjudicators.

Treorky Male Choir, 1885. They won the St Fagan's Eisteddfod on Whitsun weekend 1885 for their performance of *Comrades in Arms* where the adjudicator was Caradog, who enjoyed fame as the conductor of a 350-mixed voice choir which performed in Crystal Palace in 1872 and 1873. William Thomas was an original member, and his rival, Tom Stephens, conductor of the Rhondda Glee Society, was a boy soprano.

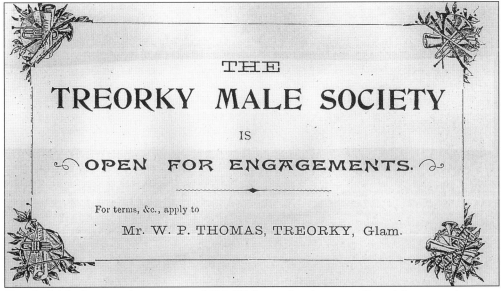

THE

TREORKY MALE SOCIETY

IS

ᓚOPEN FOR ENGAGEMENTS.ᓗ

For terms, &c., apply to

Mr. W. P. THOMAS, TREORKY, Glam.

Treorky Male Society advertisement, 1888. With membership exceeding eighty men, they won £50 at an eisteddfod in Neath before winning the Royal National Eisteddfod, Brecon, August 1889. Adjudicator Professor Atkins said it was 'The best performance I have ever heard by a male choir'. In second place was Rhondda Glee Society, fuelling the already heated rivalry between both musical organizations.

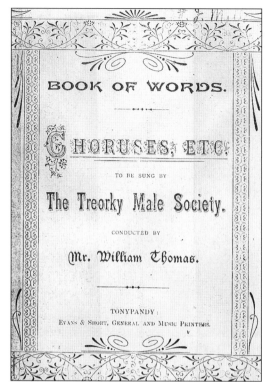

BOOK OF WORDS.

CHORUSES, ETC.

TO BE SUNG BY

The Treorky Male Society.

CONDUCTED BY

Mr. William Thomas.

TONYPANDY:
EVANS & SHORT, GENERAL AND MUSIC PRINTERS.

Book of Words of Choruses, 1890. The feud between Treorky and the Rhondda Glee Society, reached a pinnacle in the 1893 Pontypridd National Eisteddfod as the winners would go on to compete at the Chicago World Fair. At one point Treorky was ahead but the Glee Society's performance of *The Tyrol* clinched the prize. Conductor Tom Stephens received first hand information about the yodelling techniques of the Tyrolean Mountaineers from a brewery traveller who visited his tavern. The introduction of this piece of realism was the turning point in the competition and earned them the transatlantic ticket.

POST OFFICE TELEGRAPHS.

No. of Telegram.............

Office Stamp.

Eyre & Spottiswoode, London.

If the accuracy of an Inland Telegram be doubted, the telegram will be repeated on payment of half the amount originally paid for its transmission, any fraction of 1d. less than ½d. being reckoned as ½d.; and if it be found that there was any inaccuracy, the amount paid for repetition will be refunded. Special conditions are applicable to the repetition of Foreign Telegrams.

Charges to pay £ s.

O H M S

Handed in Windsor Castle   Office at 5 50 .M.   Received here at 6 40 p.M.

TO { Mr Thomas 70 Dumfries Treorchy.

The Queen has decided to hear Welsh Choir on Wednesday twentyseventh please Communicate With me as to Any Arrangements you wish made Lord Edward Clinton

Royal Command Performance Telegram, 1895. After winning the Royal National Eisteddfod in Llanelli (where each adjudicator independently wrote the word 'wonderful' and awarded them 100 points), Treorky became favourites of Lady Dunraven and made regular visits to her castle near Bridgend, also travelling to Edinburgh to entertain the Duke of Cambridge. Lady Dunraven secured this royal command, sent by Her Majesty's secretary, Lord Edward Clinton, to perform at Windsor – the date was changed because of a bereavement in the royal court.

Treorky Male Choir, 1895. Vicar of Ystradyfodwg Revd W. Lewis held open air meetings to raise funds for the choir to undertake the journey and they also gave a series of concerts in the Cardiff Panoptican Theatre. With enough money collected, they hired a fleet of rail carriages for the journey to Windsor and spent a memorable weekend in London.

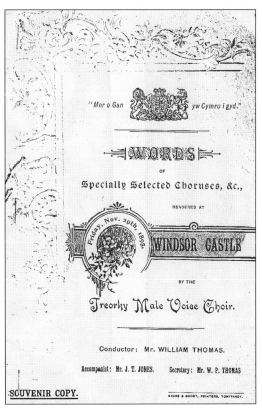

Windsor Castle Concert Programme, 1895. Composer Dr Joseph Parry accompanied the eighty members, advising them not to laugh on the train or it would affect their voices! At home, Tom Stephens was furious over the invitation and accused the postmaster of delivering the telegram to the wrong choir. In 1898 the Rhondda Glee Society performed at Windsor but did not receive the same welcome as Treorky because the choristers wore white gloves and were treated as professionals, whereas Treorky appeared in their Sunday Best and were recognized as amateurs.

An extract from Morien's *Western Mail* report, November, 1895. This newspaper coined the phrase, 'They behaved like gentlemen and sang like angels'. The concert in St George's Hall was an unparalleled success, with Her Majesty Queen Victoria, dressed in typical black veil, twice calling on William Thomas to congratulate him and ask specific questions about the content of the programme. Along with sixty guests, many of whom were members of the Royal Family, the Queen requested a number of encores; practically unheard of in the royal court.

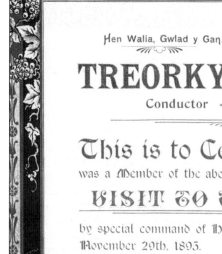

Hen Walia, Gwlad y Gan. Sain Can yw Swyn Cenedl.

TREORKY MALE CHOIR.
Conductor - Mr. WILLIAM THOMAS.

This is to Certify that Mr. *Wm Thomas (Conductor)* was a Member of the above Choir on the occasion of their

VISIT TO WINDSOR CASTLE

by special command of Her Most Gracious Majesty Queen Victoria, November 29th, 1895.

Llewelyn Williams, Pres.   W. P. Thomas, Hon. Sec.

John Bebb, Treasurer.   W. H. Owen, Financial Sec.

A Commemorative Royal Concert Certificate, 1895. During the visit, the choir enjoyed trips to London Zoo and Crystal Palace but were turned away from the House of Lords for singing too loudly outside! Returning to Treorky, they were greeted by a 'monster procession' of brass bands and 'a sea of upturned faces'. The conductor was carried shoulder high through the darkened streets before reaching the decorated lamp pillar in Stag Square where he lead the choir in a performance of *God Save The Queen, Men of Harlech* and *Hen Wlad Fy Nhadau*.

Crest of the Royal Baton, encrusted with rubies, diamonds and emeralds, which was sent to William Thomas by Her Majesty Queen Victoria to commemorate the concert. The choir held a celebratory dinner in the Drill Hall, Pentre, in 1896 but with prestigious engagements already booked and realizing the difficulties of transporting so many choristers, the conductor chose twenty-five of his best singers to form the Royal Welsh Male Choir. The last recorded existence of a Treorky Male Choir was at a competition in 1897 under the direction of John Bebb.

Gwilym T. Jones, conductor, Treorchy and District Male Voice Party, 1920-1926. The conductor of the Royal Welsh Male Choir, he also lead the Treorchy choir which was reformed in 1917 under John Pugh with Fred Hughes as accompanist. In 1924 they performed for The Duke of York at Ystradfechan Park and won a record five consecutive eisteddfodau during a weekend trip to west Wales. He was replaced by John Isaac Jones, who led them to a first prize in Pontarddulais where famed Glasgow Orpheus Choir conductor Sir Hugh Roberton was adjudicating. With the choir's main rivals Williamstown now almost defunct, a new player in the world of 'cythraul canu' was formed in Arthur Duggan's neighbouring Pendyrus.

William David Evans (conductor), Treorchy and District Male Voice Choir, 1932 – 1938. Maerdy-born 'W.D.', who trained as a schoolmaster in Goldsmiths College, London was a respected composer of hymn tunes and folk songs. His first victory with Treorchy was at the 1932 hometown semi-national eisteddfod when Arwel Hughes presented them with ninety-one points for their performance of *Charge of the Light Brigade*. They later won a choral competition at the Central Hall, Westminster and gave their first radio broadcast from the Park and Dare Theatre in October, 1935. The choir experienced major internal difficulties because members of the Royal Welsh, who occasionally made up the first two front rows, were allegedly being paid for singing while many other choristers were unemployed miners.

Treorchy Male Voice Choir, 1920. Following W.D. Evans' resignation, Arthur Davies, a 'man of culture' from Swansea took over. In September 1938 while the choir was rehearsing *Voyage of Love* two men, who would have a profound affect on its future, became deputy conductor and accompanist respectively. They were John Haydn Davies and his friend Tom Jones. It was Mr Davies who conducted them in a radio broadcast later that year, but their success was short lived as massive economic problems and wartime difficulties forced them to disband in May, 1943.

Two
Comrades in Arms
1946-1950

Your high standards have rightly earned for you recognition as one of the world's best choirs. We are proud that you are named after one of the Rhondda's best loved communities. You represent Welsh culture at its best.

The Rt Hon George Thomas, Viscount Tonypandy

Russell Square Gardens, London, 2 April 1949. On 16 October 1946 a meeting was held in Treorchy Senior School, Glyncoli Road by Tom Jenkins and George Neighbour to reform the Treorchy and District Male Choir. Local barber Stanley Jones was appointed secretary and it was agreed to invite John Haydn Davies and Tom Jones to become the new conductor and accompanist. A week later it was announced that both men had accepted and rehearsals started in November.

John Haydn Davies MBE, conductor 1946-1969, conductor emeritus 1969-1991. Peerless as a conductor – John Haydn Davies's greatest legacy – the choir, continues as a testimony to his massive contribution to the world of choral music. Born in Blaencwm, he was educated in the local school, where he also taught for thrity-five years and was later headmaster. An accomplished musician, he was conductor of Glenrhondda Colliery Choir, Blaenselsig Male Choir and Blaencwm Choral Society before accepting the invitation to conduct Treorchy – on which he firmly stamped his musical knowledge and charismatic personality. He regularly adjudicated at the National Eisteddfod, was instrumental in forming the Pontarddulais Male Choir (becoming a Life Member) and even declined the invitation to become chorusmaster of the Welsh National Opera. His time as a conductor epitomised a renaissance in Welsh choral music of which he was a major figure.

Tom Jones, accompanist 1946-1971. A quiet, unassuming man, he accompanied the Treorchy Male Choir for twenty-five years with the utmost commitment. A dedicated musician who never sought the limelight but was content to serve the choir, he was praised by adjudicators at the National Eisteddfod for his brilliant playing of the piano. Tom worked at the Park Colliery before becoming an insurance agent. He died at his home in Howard Street, Treorchy at the age of sixty-six, while still a full-time member of the choir's music staff.

Concert programme of the choir's first public performance at Ramah Chapel, Treorchy, 20 July 1947. It was here that a collection of £12 was raised for choir funds. During the first rehearsal, John Haydn Davies sang a note and told the men who could sing above it to stand to the left, the low voices to the right, and a long period of training through the tonic solfa notation began. Membership grew to more than 150 choristers and the attendance books were later closed.

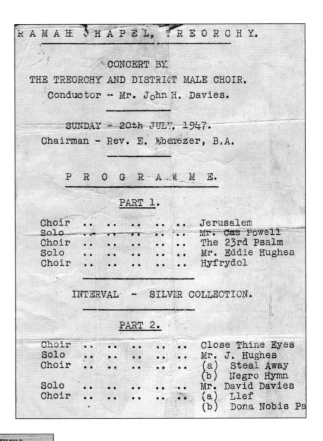

RAMAH CHAPEL, TREORCHY.

CONCERT BY

THE TREORCHY AND DISTRICT MALE CHOIR.

Conductor - Mr. John H. Davies.

SUNDAY - 20th JULY, 1947.

Chairman - Rev. E. Ebenezer, B.A.

PROGRAMME.

PART 1.

Choir	.. ..	Jerusalem
Solo	.. ..	Mr. Cas Powell
Choir	.. ..	The 23rd Psalm
Solo	.. ..	Mr. Eddie Hughes
Choir	.. ..	Hyfrydol

INTERVAL - SILVER COLLECTION.

PART 2.

Choir	.. ..	Close Thine Eyes
Solo	.. ..	Mr. J. Hughes
Choir	.. ..	(a) Steal Away
		(b) Negro Hymn
Solo	.. ..	Mr. David Davies
Choir	.. ..	(a) Llef
		(b) Dona Nobis Pa

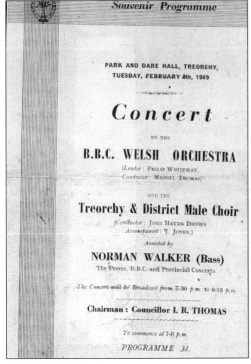

Souvenir Programme

PARK AND DARE HALL, TREORCHY,
TUESDAY, FEBRUARY 8th, 1949

Concert

BY THE

B.B.C. WELSH ORCHESTRA

(Leader : PHILIP WHITEWAY.
Conductor : MANSEL THOMAS)

AND THE

Treorchy & District Male Choir

(Conductor : JOHN HAYDN DAVIES
Accompanist : T. JONES.)

Assisted by

NORMAN WALKER (Bass)

The Proms, B.B.C. and Provincial Concerts.

The Concert will be Broadcast from 7-30 p.m. to 8-15 p.m.

Chairman : Councillor I. R. THOMAS

To commence at 7-0 p.m.

PROGRAMME 3d.

Concert Programme, 9 February 1949. The choir held its first celebrity concert in Bethlehem Chapel, Treorchy on 1 April 1948, with Linda Parker and William Parsons as soloists. The composer of *Close Thine Eyes*, Ieuan Rees, came on stage to conduct the item. The choir also began to appreciate the talent of their young baritone soloist, Sam Griffiths who made his debut performance in July of the same year.

Herald of Wales, 26 February 1949. The choir appeared before HRH The Duke of Edinburgh at Wembley Pool, London for the NCB Boxing Finals owing to a friendship with press officer Fred Pullin. Dressed in overalls and wearing helmet and cap lamp, the 150 members filed into their seats almost unnoticed. The lights were extinguished and they turned on the lamps, with a gasp of admiration from the audience of 10,000 people. The conductor was presented to the Duke following the performance.

Russell Square Gardens, London, 2 April 1949, prior to the NCB Boxing Finals. In October 1948, the choir made its first broadcast in a BBC programme called *Export Only* from the Reardon Smith Lecture Theatre, Cardiff and received £15 15s 0d in fees. A few months later the choir reached 170 members, but according to the committee's minute book, '18 were told their membership ceased and the future of another 54 will be decided shortly.' Today, membership remains in the region of 120 choristers.

First edition of *Excelsior: The Voice of the Treorchy and District Male Choir*. In April 1948 committee member William Wiltshire proposed for a monthly pamphlet to be printed on the activities of the choir with Keri Williams, Richard Williams, Ernest Lewis and W.J. 'Donna' Griffiths producing it. According to Donna, the title was 'chosen because it was the essence of an idea of something almost impossible to attain'. *Excelsior* appeared quarterly, for the sum of 3d a copy and in 1953 became an annual publication. To date more than 25,000 copies have been issued throughout the world.

National Eisteddfod, Dolgellau, 6 August 1949. The choir's first competition entry was at the Whitsun Semi-National Eisteddfod in Treorchy, May 1948. They won the second prize on the test piece *Nidaros*, remembering John Haydn Davies's immortal words, 'If you lose say little, if you win say less.' For the first national entry in Dolgellau, the choir won second prize for their performance of *Mordaith Cariad*, *Tiger Tiger* and *Full Fathom Five*. Following the adjudication on all five contestants, the Treorchy conductor said, 'Our object is not to gain a prize or to defeat a rival, but to pace one another on the road to excellence.'

Treorchy and District Male Choir's first official photograph, 1949. Choristers made their first continental connection in January 1950 when they performed on the BBC *Choral Exchange* with three French choirs in Lille. During the victorious Llanharan Semi-National Eisteddfod in May, adjudicator Alan Bush, Professor of Composition at the

Royal Academy of Music, London presented the choir with his choral work, *Owain Glyndwr*, which he dedicated to them. In August 1950 they won the second prize at the National Eisteddfod, Caerphilly.

W.J. 'Donna' Griffiths, publicity officer 1948-1952; secretary 1952-1980; vice chairman 1980-1981; chairman 1981. His record of dedicated service to the choir is without equal and he remains an inspiring example to all who followed him. The headmaster of Porth Junior School, he was active in the Trade Union Movement and deacon of Bodringallt Welsh Independent Chapel. He once said: 'It is more than just a choir, it is a fellowship.'

Iorwerth Thomas, president 1948-1966. Councillor Thomas, later MP for the Rhondda in 1950, was appointed the first president. He assisted in the early years of the choir's development and proudly spoke of 'his choir' at the House of Commons. Other candidates included Ocean Coal Company executive W.P. Thomas, the company's general manager Levi Phillips and J.J. Thomas, a local wine merchant and 'sole agent for Bulmer's Cider.' For his contribution to promoting music in the community Tom Jenkins, who was blind, was appointed vice president and became the choir's first Life Member.

Three

Calon Lan
1951-1960

I'll never forget hearing Nidaros. Boys bach, it was wonderful. Come to think of it, I would give up the caps for playing for Wales if only I had the ability to be the conductor of The Treorchy.

Cliff Morgan

Ipswich, 7 July 1951. The choir enjoyed a weekend visit to Ipswich and performed in Christchurch Park and later in the town's Coal Exchange with the Ipswich Youth Singers and choir soloists Sam Griffiths and Idris Higgon. Earlier in the year they made a radio broadcast with well-known comedian Wilfred Pickles.

Annual Dinner, Polikoff Assembly Hall with composer Mansel Thomas, radio presenter Alun Williams, Alwyn Jones, Fred Pullin (NCB) and Mr Luke (Polikoffs), three years after the first dinner was held in the British Legion Hall, Pentre. Firm friendships were secured with both of these influential BBC broadcasters and musicians along with composer Arwel Hughes who would remain a close colleague for many years.

Festival of Britain, 12 May 1951, featuring the four Morgan brothers of Mal, Islwyn, Jack and David. The choir travelled to London to perform a Festival of Britain concert in the Royal Albert Hall under the direction of Sir Adrian Boult. Entitled *The Rainbow* it was based on the evacuation of Dunkirk. Treorchy joined eleven other choirs and six brass bands for the mass performance with soloists Jan Van Der and Maurice Bevan. They performed it again on 11 November 1951 at Polikoff Hall, with the Cory Band.

Christchurch Park Festival Fête, Ipswich, 7 July 1951. Although entitled the Treorchy and District Male Choir, the organization was still known locally as 'The Party'. A choir badge was designed by one of the choristers and plans were afoot to rename it the Treorchy Male Choir.

British Foreign Secretary, The Rt Hon Herbert Morrison MP, Ipswich, 7 July 1951. The choir spent a weekend in Ipswich where they were honoured with a civic reception before performing in Christchurch Park for thousands of visitors. Mr Morrison asked the choir to sing a few impromptu songs for his guests and they performed *Cwm Rhondda, Llef* and *Aberystwyth*.

Birmingham Town Hall, 20 October 1951. A convoy of eight coaches carried 300 choristers and supporters for the choir's debut performance in the Town Hall organized by the Birmingham Welsh Society. The concert stage was shared with soprano Ruth Packer and bass-baritone Bruce Dargrave.

Altogether BBC radio broadcast with Alun Williams at the rehearsal room, 1951. The only choir to have its own radio show, they made thirty-two *Altogether* broadcasts, which consisted of ninety-three student songs, sea shanties, spirituals and Welsh airs – many of which were only available four days before the live broadcast. On one occasion Mr Williams was driving over the Rhigos Mountain and heard the live radio programme begin, knowing full well he would not reach the school in time!

OFFICIALS :

Chairman .... Mr. J. G. Neighbour
Vice-Chairman ...... Mr. E. Knapgate
Secretary .... Mr. W. J. Griffiths
Treasurer .... Mr. Gwynne Williams
Librarian .... Mr. Cly. Willis
Assist. Librarian ... Mr. Emrys Thomas
Registrar .... Mr. Idris Thomas
Contrib. Secretary ... Mr. Elwyn Jones

COMMITTEE

Messrs.

D. J. Davies	Will Jones
Eddie Davies	Richie Lewis
Emlyn Davies	Trevor Protheroe
Dan Edwards	H. J. Thatcher

Victory Souvenir

**ROYAL NATIONAL
EISTEDDFOD
OF WALES**

Aberystwyth, August 9th, 1952

Treorchy Male Choir

President :
Mr. IORWERTH R. THOMAS, M.P.

Vice-President :
Mr. TOM J. JENKINS.

Conductor :
Mr. JOHN DAVIES.

Accompanist : Mr. TOM JONES

Commemorative Scorecard, Royal National Eisteddfod of Wales, Aberystwyth 1952. The adjudicators were so overwhelmed by the choir's performance of *Schubert's 23 Psalm, Duw Yw Fy Mugail*, that they all placed their notebooks and pencils down to listen. On awarding the choir their first win at the national event, Chief Adjudicator W. Matthew Williams said, 'It is only once in a century one hears such marvellous singing which was so moving that tears came into my eyes. If there is singing like this in heaven, then I am eager to get there quickly'. It was a glorious chapter in the history of the choir.

Treorchy and District Male Choir, 1952. In December they made recordings of Welsh airs which were sent to Bethlehem, Pittsburg, USA and buried in a time capsule for a hundred years. The first uniform of blazer and greys was issued at a total cost of £3 10s 0d each, of which the choristers paid £2. They first wore them in Maesteg Town Hall in February 1953 and it was also the first time for Brewer's Bus Company to transport them to a venue. They remained the regular choir coach company for more than forty years.

Treorchy Male Choir in rehearsals, 1953. Even today choristers stand for the duration of the ninety minute 'practice' held twice a week, and learn through the tonic solfa musical notation. In November 1953 they appeared at the Royal Festival Hall with Geraint Evans and Osian Ellis for the London Welsh Society's Autumn Concert and performed at the premier of *A Valley of Song* at the Queen's Cinema, Cardiff.

Sailing up the Kyles of Bute in Scotland to the village of Tinnabruach on board the steamer, *Queen Mary II* during the Glasgow weekend, May 1953. Due to the friendship that existed between John Haydn Davies and the late Sir Hugh Roberton of the Glasgow Orpheus Choir, an association began between Treorchy and Farquhar MacDonald, conductor of the Glasgow Police Choir and a former member of the Orpheus. In 1953 Treorchy undertook a tour of Glasgow, performing two combined concerts in St Andrew's Hall.

Outside the Red Cow Hotel, Treorchy, 5 June 1954. The Glasgow Police Choir was reunited with the Treorchy choristers during a weekend visit to the Rhondda where they performed a combined concert in the Park and Dare Theatre.

Gower Coast Trip with the Glasgow Police Choir, 5 June 1954. During the weekend visit, the Glasgow and Treorchy choristers enjoyed a day trip to the Mumbles and Gower. Despite the pouring rain there was always a pub nearby!

A celebratory night with the Glasgow Police Choir, June 1954. Conductor Farquhar MacDonald said it was 'a climax in the life of our choir, because we have established something much deeper than the love of music – we have established a bond of friendship with the salt of the earth – Treorchy'.

Celebrating the first prize at the National Eisteddfod, Ystradgynlais, 7 August 1954. Now officially named Treorchy Male Choir, choristers made their first television programme, *Easter Parade* under the baton of Arwel Hughes, accompanied by the Welsh Variety Orchestra.

**ROYAL NATIONAL
EISTEDDFOD OF WALES**

YSTRADGYNLAIS - 1954

GOLD MOUNTED BATON
AND GOLD MEDAL

presented to Mr.

John Haydn Davies

CONDUCTOR OF WINNING CHOIR
(Treorchy Male Choir)

in

CHIEF MALE
CHORAL COMPETITION

Royal National Eisteddfod of Wales Ystradgynlais Certificate, 7 August 1954. Treorchy beat Pendyrus, conductor Arthur Duggan, by five points on the test pieces *Nidaros*, *Henffych Gorff* and *Salm Bywyd*. The unique 'Treorchy tone' was fully nurtured and developed by the conductor in these early days, creating the choir's distinctly smooth tenor sound which can still be called their own and a quality many others have attempted to imitate.

Rehearsal Room, 1954. On 1 March 1955 they performed a St David's Day concert in Sophia Gardens, Cardiff with the BBC Orchestra, Mervyn John, Hugh Griffiths, Rachel Thomas, Donald Houston and Petula Clark. Sportsmen John Brackway, Dai Dower and Wilfred Wooler were also present for the occasion along with the Archdeacon of Wales and the Father of the House of Commons.

Cherubini Requiem Programme, 24 November 1955. The artistic climax of the choir in the early years was attained at the first performance in the Rhondda of the *Cherubini Requiem* in St Peter's church, Pentre. To perform such an extended work, in Latin and without copies, was a credit to John Haydn Davies for his brilliant tuition and the perseverance of the choristers.

John Haydn Davies in rehearsals, 1956. Despite giving a public performance of each test item prior to a National Eisteddfod, the final rehearsal was always a private event. The rehearsal room continues to welcome guests from throughout the world. This picture was taken prior to the choir's performance in the Olympia Cinema, Cardiff for the world premier of *Helen of Troy* starring Rhondda actor Stanley Baker and Brigitte Bardot.

National Eisteddfod, Aberdare, 11 August 1956. For the choir's third consecutive national eisteddfod win, they beat Morriston Orpheus Male Choir for the first time. Earlier in the year the choir appeared in a film about Wales for the Walt Disney Film Company which was shown in the USA at Christmas time and also made a return weekend visit to Ipswich.

National Eisteddfod, Aberdare, 11 August 1956. On 6 October the choir won the first of five consecutive entries in the Miners' Eisteddfod, held at the Pavillion in Porthcawl. It is also interesting to note that at that time, of the 115 singing members of the choir, 28 of them were related and the average age was twenty-five.

National Eisteddfod, Aberdare, 11 August 1956. Treorchy scored 274 points, above Morriston's 268 and Pendyrus' 258 on the test pieces Y *Gwyntoedd, Mawr Arglwydd* and *Dydd Da Fy Mherl*. Although the choir was large enough to compete in the chief male choral section, they were usually the smallest choir on stage, taking full advantage of the exquisite pianissimo phrases with their unique tone.

Treorchy Male Choir, 1956. This photograph commemorates the tenth anniversary of the choir since re-formation in 1946. The choir's popularity was rapidly increasing, largely due to the huge demand for radio broadcasts which were usually recorded in the rehearsal room on Glyncoli Road, or Polikoff's factory canteen.

Welsh Teledisc Sleeve of *Martyrs of the Arena* and *The Crusaders*. The choir made its first commercial recording, a 78rpm Qualiton Record, at Bethlehem Chapel, Treorchy on 23 February 1956, featuring *Sospan Fach* and *Harlech*. Another four records were made and issued during the year. The choir's recording of *Sospan Fach* was later used as the signature tune of BBC Radio Wales' popular Saturday programme, *Sports Review* for more than thirty years. Unfortunately the choir had no royalty rights over it.

Rehearsal Room, 1957. From left to right: Dicky Fear, Wally Breeze, Ron Dowling (who collapsed prior to a concert in Ross-on-Wye some years later and died without regaining consciousness), Mike Gale, Mel Davies, Idris Thomas and Ben Jackson.

Cardigan Semi National Eisteddfod, 19 May 1957. The choir scored 182 points over Beaufort's 176 and Pendyrus' 175 on the test pieces *Salm Bywyd* and *Dydd Da Fy Mherl*. Both Pendyrus and Treorchy, situated within miles of each other, had long since developed a mutual admiration and friendly rivalry.

Cardigan Semi National Eisteddfod, 19 May 1957. Treorchy has remained a registered charity for decades and even today the majority of its concerts are in aid of worthy causes. Choristers continue to spend wintry nights carol singing around the valley to raise funds, or to entertain the elderly members of the community.

One of the choir's first long-player recordings. To mark the 100th record made by Qualiton in October 1958, managing director John Edwards invited them to record *Hen Wlad Fy Nhadau* and *God Bless The Prince of Wales* and within sixteen hours it was on sale in the Cardiff shops. This was recognized as the shortest making-selling time of any record.

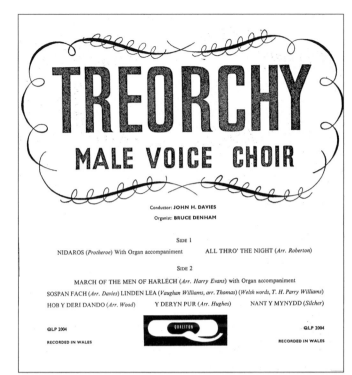

TREORCHY

MALE VOICE CHOIR

Conductor: **JOHN H. DAVIES**
Organist: **BRUCE DENHAM**

Side 1

NIDAROS (*Protheroe*) With Organ accompaniment   ALL THRO' THE NIGHT (*Arr. Roberton*)

Side 2

MARCH OF THE MEN OF HARLECH (*Arr. Harry Evans*) with Organ accompaniment
SOSPAN FACH (*Arr. Davies*) LINDEN LEA (*Vaughan Williams, arr. Thomas*) (*Welsh words, T. H. Parry Williams*)
HOB Y DERI DANDO (*Arr. Wood*)   Y DERYN PUR (*Arr. Hughes*)   NANT Y MYNYDD (*Silcher*)

QLP 2004   QALITON   QLP 2004

RECORDED IN WALES   RECORDED IN WALES

Gelli Colliery, 2 November 1957. To commemorate the twenty-first birthday of the television programme *The World Our Stage*, the choir appeared with the Scottish Junior Singers from Edinburgh, the Royal Choral Society and the London Symphony Orchestra. It was a tripartite regional link-up, with choirs and orchestras performing in their own localities. Treorchy performed from a wet, muddy Gelli Colliery with John Davies standing on top of an old oil drum!

TREORCHY MALE CHOIR

DINNER and DANCE

AT PARK HOTEL, CARDIFF
On Saturday, January 19th, 1957

6.30 p.m. for 7 p.m.

To preside - G. J. NEIGHBOUR, Esq.
(Chairman of Choir).

Dinner and Dance Menu, Cardiff 1957. Each year the choir would invite guest speakers to join them for this prestigious event, but in recognition of their support, the chief guests of the 1959 dinner were the wives of the choristers! Due to the enormous dedication shown by choristers and patience of their partners, it has often been suggested that wedding vows in the Rhondda are changed to: 'Do you take this man AND the Treorchy Male Choir.'

Miners Eisteddfod Record, 5 October 1957. The choir exchanged greetings in song on a transatlantic link from the Miners' Eisteddfod, Porthcawl with singer Paul Robeson who was in a studio in New York. More than forty years later the remaining choristers who performed on this special day met Paul Robeson Jnr on his visit to the Rhondda.

MLP 3001

MANUFACTURED FOR
N.U.M. (SOUTH WALES AREA)
BY CWALITON RECORDS
(WALES) LTD.

TRANSATLANTIC EXCHANGE

★

Paul Robeson IN NEW YORK

THE MINERS' EISTEDDFOD AT PORTHCAWL
SATURDAY, OCTOBER 5th, 1957

PAUL ROBESON singing
DID'N MY LORD DELIVER DANIEL? · ALL THROUGH THE NIGHT
THE LITTLE LIGHT OF MINE · ALL MEN ARE BROTHERS
SCHUBERT'S LULLABY

THE TREORCHY MALE VOICE CHOIR singing
Y DELYN AUR · WE'LL KEEP A WELCOME IN THE HILLSIDE

N.U.M. | LONG PLAYING RECORD

Festival Hall poster, 7 December 1957. Appearing in the Royal Festival Hall, London, the choir hired a 'musical express' to carry 500 supporters and choristers to the performance. Among the artists were Siân Phillips and Gwyneth Jones.

TREORCHY MALE CHOIR
Concert at the ROYAL FESTIVAL HALL
SATURDAY, DECEMBER 7th, 1957
SPECIAL TRAIN TO
LONDON
(PADDINGTON)

Through Train from Treherbert, Treorchy, Ystrad Lwynypia, Tonypandy, Dinas & Porth

☞ TWELVE HOURS in LONDON.   Specially quoted Fare - 29/

FORWARD			RETURN		
Treherbert	dep.	7.10 a.m.	Paddington	dep.	12.35 a.m
Treorchy	,,	7.15 a.m.	Porth	arr.	4.42 a.m
Ystrad	,,	7.20 a.m.	Dinas	,,	4.49 a.m
Llwynypia	,,	7.25 a.m.	Tonypandy	,,	4.53 a.m
Tonypandy	,,	7.30 a.m.	Llwynypia	,,	4.58 a.m
Dinas	,,	7.35 a.m.	Ystrad	,,	5.03 a.m
Porth	,,	7.40 a.m.	Treorchy	,,	5.06 a.m
Paddington	arr.	11.50 a.m.	Treherbert	,,	5.15 a.m

Tickets **NOT** available from British Railways, but can be obtained at Choir Rehearsals, The County Secondary School, Glyncoli Road, Treorchy on Tuesdays and Thursday, 7.30 - 9 p.m., and Sundays, 3.30 - 5 p.m. or from The Secretary, Mr. W. J. GRIFFITHS, 26 Glyncoli Road, Treorchy.

Take this splendid opportunity to visit friends or relative ☞ West End Theatres, or the Royal Festival Hall. ◄

On stage at the Festival Hall, London, 7 December 1957. A few days later the choir cut the first of eight extended-play records with the popular Qualiton Label of Pontardawe.

Rehearsal Room, 1958. On 6 February 1958 the choir performed in Trerhondda Chapel, Ferndale with young tenor Stuart Burrows, who was celebrating his twenty-sixth birthday on the following day. In years to come the Cilfynydd-born singer would become recognized as one of the leading operatic tenors of his generation. A few months later the choir had the distinction of appearing in the first Llandaff Festival of Music where they performed *Cherubini's Requiem*.

National Eisteddfod, Ebbw Vale, 9 August 1958. The choir's fourth consecutive national win was against Pendyrus and Beaufort on the test pieces *Y Rhaeadr* and *Angladd y Marchog*. Earlier that summer they performed direct from the British Empire and Commonwealth Games in St Athans on a broadcast called *Friday Night is Commonwealth Night* with the BBC Welsh Orchestra and presenter Wynford Vaughn Thomas.

Ebbw Vale National Eisteddfod Certificate, 1958. On 19 January 1959 they performed in the New Theatre, Cardiff for the memorial concert of Ivor Novello, with Olive Gilbert, Esme Lewis, Ivor Emmanuel and the Orchestra of the Welsh Guards. They also made a return visit to the Royal Albert Hall.

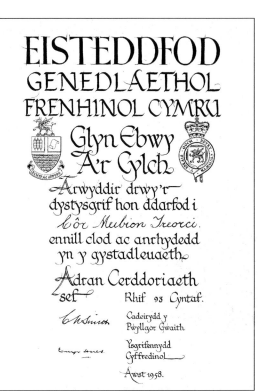

Returning from the National Eisteddfod, Ebbw Vale, 9 August 1958. In June 1959 the choir gave the first performance of *Praise Ye The Lord*, composed by Mansel Thomas and dedicated to them, at Llandaff Cathedral.

National Eisteddfod, Caernarfon, 8 August 1959. This was a very competitive occasion because it was a straight north *v.* south event, with Rhos Orpheus, Rhosllanerchgrugog and Pendyrus Male Choirs as the other entries. Treorchy gained the first prize – their fifth consecutive win, which beat Morriston Orpheus Choir's record of four.

Caernarfon National Eisteddfod, 8 August 1959. The choir performed *Matona* and *Cadlef Y Weriniaeth* for an estimated audience of 29,000 people inside and outside the marquee. At the Miners' Eisteddfod, Porthcawl in September, they became the first choir in the UK to perform the *Coronation Scene* from *Boris Godounov* in English. The soloist was their talented baritone, Sam Griffiths.

Treorchy Male Choir, 1959. A firm friendship developed between John Haydn Davies and the subsequent conductor of Pendyrus Male Choir, Glynne Jones, who considered himself as Treorchy's 'prince in waiting'. Following the Caernarfon Eisteddfod, Mr Jones and a group of slightly inebriated choristers, dressed in bardic robes made out of bed clothes, convened a mock Eisteddfod Court on the Menai Straits. On the following day he returned to his Ford Prefect to find a partially finished headstone reading 'Er Cof Glynne Jones' on the passenger's seat – prophetic as far as his future with Treorchy was concerned.

Treorchy Male Choir on their way to Ipswich, 23 April 1960. During the year the choir's sporting connections were strengthened when they performed at the Diving Championships of Scotland, Ireland and Wales at the Empire Pool, Cardiff.

Mayor of Ipswich, Dick Lewis, St Mathew's Bath Hall on April 23, 1960. Dick was born in the Rhondda and was a member of the valley's Urban Council in the 1920s and is seen here making a presentation to John Haydn Davies during the choir's visit.

Market Hall, Brecon, 29 May 1960. Rain almost stopped play because of the noise on the tin roof above! The choir performed in a Civic Sunday Service for the town mayor, J.V.C. Thomas who was originally from Cwmparc. Following the concert they travelled to the Welfare Hall, Tumble for the second engagement of the day.

Four
Glory and Love
1961-1970

I have never been so moved as I was by the performance of the Treorchy Male Choir. They are a great bunch of lads and I'm proud to have been associated with them.

Sir Harry Secombe

Treorchy Male Choir, Rhigos Mountain, Rhondda, 8 June 1969. The choir were filming a performance of *The Minstral Boy* for the *Choirs of the World* feature film by a German production company.

A publicity picture taken to commemorate the choir's win at the National Eisteddfod, Rhosllanerchgrugog, 12 August 1961. It was a straight competition between Treorchy and Morriston Orpheus Choir on the test pieces *Y Regali* and *Nidaros*. On Elgar's piece, Treorchy, who sang second, achieved a climax half way through that brought the premature applause from a rapt audience. At that moment the 28,000 spectators knew John Haydn Davies's choir were ahead.

First prize certificate for the National Eisteddfod, Rhosllanerchgrugog, 12 August 1961. This victory set an all-time record of six consecutive wins at the national event against the other fellow 'Giants' of choral music. The choir's magnificent, unbeaten, run of consecutive national wins came to an abrupt end in 1962 with a second place at Llanelli. Typically, John Haydn Davies was the first man on stage to congratulate the winning choir's conductor.

Rhosllanerchgrugog National Eisteddfod winners, 12 August 1961. On being awarded 183 points, the adjudicator said, 'The conductor is an artist, playing on his choir with skilful hands, drawing from them melodious music and all sublime in style.'

Herald of Wales newspaper picture of the choir's win at the Rhosllanerchgrugog National Eisteddfod, 12 August 1961. During the following month the choir made a return visit to the RAF St Athan to commemorate the anniversary of the Battle of Britain.

Back home following the trip to the National Eisteddfod in Rhosllanerchgrugog, 12 August 1961. With almost 350 concert engagements performed in the last fifteen years, their demand for TV and radio broadcasts was reaching an all-time high during this decade.

John Haydn Davies accompanied by his wife Olwen and children Susan and Geraint, Buckingham Palace, August 1961. He was being awarded the MBE by Her Majesty The Queen. Seldom has the honour been more richly deserved or widely acclaimed.

Wales *v*. England Football Programme, 14 October 1961. The choir, accompanied by the Mid Rhondda Workmen's Band, performed for the crowd at Ninian Park, Cardiff. John Haydn Davies was invited to lead the congregational singing on a number of occasions at these special events.

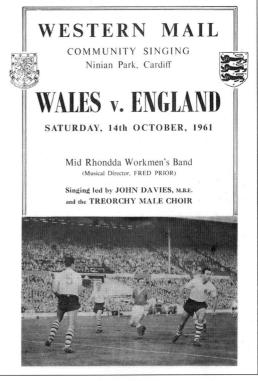

WESTERN MAIL
COMMUNITY SINGING
Ninian Park, Cardiff

WALES v. ENGLAND

SATURDAY, 14th OCTOBER, 1961

Mid Rhondda Workmen's Band
(Musical Director, FRED PRIOR)

Singing led by JOHN DAVIES, M.B.E.
and the TREORCHY MALE CHOIR

Choristers, from left to right: Eddie Rowe, Tom Thomas ('Tommy Twice'), Alun Morgan, Ray Williams, Cliff Chislett and Erfyl Lewis on Park Colliery, 1963. A publicity shot to raise awareness of the choir's tour to Switzerland following an invitation by the National Coal Board and the Coal Industry Social Welfare Organization.

Publicity photograph arranged by the National Coal Board, rehearsal room, Switzerland, 1963.
The Switzerland Tour was the choir's first overseas tour and choristers would have to wait more
than seventeen years before the next trip abroad.

Switzerland Tour official picture, September 1963. Renamed the Treorchy Miner's Choir for
the NCB sponsored trip, the choir performed seven engagements on the five-day visit for the
Federation of British Industries Fair. The first open-air performance was at the Assersihlanlage
Park.

Boarding the aeroplane for Switzerland, 7 September 1963. Following an official send-off from Stag Square by Rhondda Borough Council Mayor John Gwyn, the entire tour was filmed by the NCB. During the visit they performed in Baden-Baden, Schaffhausen, Winterthur and in the Lord Mayor's procession, Zurich before a crowd of 85,000 people.

Marching through Zurich, Switzerland, 8 September 1963. Dressed in NCB overalls, boots and helmets, they assembled at the Military Barracks and moved off with the procession with John Haydn Davies in front, waving his baton above his head. The evening concert was in the city's beautiful St Andrew's church.

Marching through Zurich, Switzerland, 8 September 1963. Apparently while the choir was passing the enormous crowds they heard a man with a distinct Welsh accent shout 'I've heard better singing in The Stag in Treorchy!' During the trip they also enjoyed visits to the top of the 7,000ft Mount Pilatus by Funicular Railways Cable Car and the lake-side town of Lucere.

Treorchy choristers Dicky Fear, Cas Powell, Eilir Wright, Haydn Erasmus and Donna Griffiths in Switzerland, September 1963. The choir was accompanied by a military band at the Kongresshalle before a packed audience numbering in excess of 3,000 people. By the end of the tour, one chorister had bought so many Swiss clocks and watches he was forever more nicknamed Dai 'Tick-Tock'.

Shauffhausen Rhine Falls, 9 September 1963. The choir performed in the main square of the town, where hundreds of people turned out, some standing on balconies to enjoy an evening of beautiful serenading. Naturally, singing resumed on the aeroplane journey back to London, a tradition which remains today despite poor acoustics and altitude – although such shortcomings are often ignored after plenty of 'duty free' is consumed!

Atlantic College, St Donats, 15 September 1963. The choir undertook this engagement the day after returning from their tour of Switzerland and because the weather was so warm, choristers were told to remove their jackets to sing. This was the choir's busiest year to date, with a total of fifty-three performances.

Sam Griffiths, baritone soloist 1948-1988. His period of service as a soloist has been unsurpassed and is an example in terms of musicianship and dedication. Sam, the manager of Compton Webb factory and member of Mdm Danford George's Ton Pentre Amateur Operatic Society, featured on many of the choir's commercial recordings and has performed with distinction in the choir's forays into the Eisteddfod arena. His solo performance in the *Coronation Scene* from *Boris Goudonov* revealed his artistry and ability in one of the most demanding of operatic roles.

Accompanist Tom Jones receiving the Welsh Guards Cup from Alun Williams at the National Eisteddfod, Swansea, 8 August 1964. On the Saturday prior to the competition, disaster struck when John Haydn Davies was taken ill. The final rehearsals were cancelled and the choristers did not know if they were able to compete. The event was dubbed the *Battle of the Giants* because it was the first time that the major choirs of Pontarddulais, Pendyrus, Morriston Orpheus, Manselton, Rhosllanerchrugog and Treorchy had entered the competition together.

Victory at the National Eisteddfod, Swansea, 8 August 1964. On the morning of the competition John Haydn Davies courageously left his sick bed and was driven straight to the marquee. It was in a weak, trembling condition that the maestro stood before the choir. The discipline and determination shown by each singer, especially during the last test piece *Prospice* when his gestures were imprecise, was a wonderful display of their faith in him. Treorchy won the event.

Battle of Britain Concert, Park and Dare Theatre, Treorchy, 16 September 1964. Guest conductor Alwyn Jones of the BBC, who replaced John Haydn Davies while he recovered from his illness, (along with chorister Cas Powell on occasions) was welcomed to the concert by chairman Edward Knapgate. Mr Davies' absence from the choir showed how much they had depended on him and it was all the more apparent that they needed to ease the burden he had borne for so many years.

John Haydn Davies with the winning National Eisteddfod cup, 1964. Following his return to the rehearsal room, the conductor expressed his delight at receiving the Ivor Sims Medallion donated in honour of him and awarded for the first time to the conductor of the winning choir at the eisteddfod. The two great musical directors had been friends for almost thirty years.

Coventry Central Hall with the City of Coventry Band, 7 November 1964. Only a few months later the choir entertained HRH Princess Marina, the Duchess of Kent in an engagement for the Order of St John of Jerusalem at the College of Advanced Technology, Cardiff. The choir also started a long association with the Doncaster Wheatsheaf Girls Choir following a concert in Noddfa Chapel, Treorchy.

Choristers who appeared in the first concert in Ramah Chapel, Treorchy 1947 are gathered in the rehearsal room in 1965. The choir later appeared with Gwyneth Jones at the celebrity concert at Cardigan National Eisteddfod and in September, performed at the launch of BBC2 in the Memorial Hall, Barry with Geraint Evans, Osian Ellis, the BBC Welsh Orchestra and Donald Houston.

Acton Town Hall, London, 30 October 1965. Due to the illness of John Haydn Davies the previous year, it was decided to appoint John Cynan Jones, Head of Music at Pentre Grammar School, as the choir's deputy conductor – and part-time chorister in the second bass section. He is seen here following his first engagement during a weekend visit to Ealing. He conducted his first home concert in the Park and Dare Theatre on Good Friday with the Park and Dare Band, bandmaster Ieuan Morgan. The Good Friday concert remains a popular annual event.

The official picture to commemorate the Royal Concert, 22 November 1966. Treorchy became the first Welsh choir to appear at the Festival of St Cecilia in the presence of Her Majesty the Queen and HRH The Duke of Edinburgh at the Royal Albert Hall. They were accompanied by the Bournemouth Symphony Orchestra, conductor Constantine Silvester.

Departing for the Royal Concert at the Royal Albert Hall, 22 November 1966. Following this outstandingly successful concert, long since remembered as one of the best performances ever given by the choir, conductor John Haydn Davies, chairman Edward Knapgate, accompanist Tom Jones and secretary W.J. 'Donna' Griffiths were presented to the Royal couple.

Clifford Taylor, president 1967-1998. Following the death of MP Iorwerth Thomas, Mr Taylor, from Barry, was appointed his successor. A chartered accountant, who became the managing director of Polikoff International at Ynyswen, he was of great assistance to the choir. Not only did he arrange for the choristers to obtain their first official uniform, but regularly allowed them use of the Polikoff canteen for functions, concerts and broadcasts. He served the choir diligently as its esteemed figurehead for the next thirty-ones years.

John Cynan Jones, conductor 1969-1991, conductor emeritus since 1991. Born in Pentre and educated at Pentre Primary School and Rhondda County School, John Cynan won a State Scholarship to University College, Aberystwyth, graduating with a BA in Music in 1954 and the degree of Master of Music. He won the Open Competition in Organ Playing at the National Eisteddfod and conducted the College Madrigal Singers at an International Students' Congress. An Associate of the Trinity College of Music, he was organist at the Garrison Churches of Catterick and with the B.A.O.R. at Hilden, Germany. Apart from seven years as Head of Music at Cyfarthfa Grammar School in Merthyr Tydfil, John spent all his career living and working in the Rhondda. He retired due to ill-health in 1991 as Academic Registrar of Treorchy Comprehensive School and conductor of Treorchy Male Choir.

Brangwyn Hall, Swansea, 7 April 1968. John Cynan lead them to his first win at the Semi National Eisteddfod in Cardigan, May 1967 and when Tom Jones became ill later in the year, music student Marion Williams was called upon to accompany the choir at the National Eisteddfod in Bala. When the choir was awarded first prize, she was also congratulated by the adjudicators. With the ever-increasing demand of TV programmes, recordings, concerts and changing social habits with differing holiday periods, it was decided to bring all competition work to an end. The choir had gained twenty-two 'firsts' out of twenty-seven competition entries.

Filming *Tydi a Roddaist* with an early morning dawn for *Choirs of the World* in Neath Abbey, 7 June 1969. In January John Haydn Davies officially announced his retirement as conductor after twenty-three years and more than 500 engagements. Every chorister was aware of the great loss suffered with the news and he was later made conductor emeritus of the choir. At the Annual General Meeting, on 9 February 1969, John Cynan Jones was appointed the choir's second conductor since re-formation.

Filming *Loch Lomond*, with Sam Griffiths as soloist for *Choirs of the World* in Cardiff Castle, 14 June 1969. Treorchy was chosen as one of the three greatest choirs in the world (along with Vienna Boys and the Mormon Tabernacle Choir) to appear in the Lutz Wellnitz production of this German feature film. Taking two weekends to complete, they also recorded *Hen Ferchetan* at St Fagan's Welsh Folk Museum and *Greensleeves* on the Brecon Beacons, where John Cynan fell and was taken to hospital.

Filming *Choirs of the World* during a sunset on Rhossilli Beach, 7 June 1969 before the bay went dark and choristers were stuck on the sands without a torch in sight! Some of the other venues for filming included the grounds of Penrice Castle, Oxwich Bay for a performance of *Robin Ddiog* and *The Dashing White Sergeant* in Dumfries Street, Treorchy. Members of the public saw the final product in a special screening at the Park and Dare Theatre, Treorchy.

Tom Jones buying a round of drinks at the end of a long day of filming in Borehamwood ATV Studios, Elstree, 23 November 1969. The choir was invited to spend four days in London to record his Christmas show, *This is Tom Jones*, along with Millicent Martin, Joan Collins and David Fry.

His manager, Gordon Mills, suggested Treorchy for the programme and it was left to Ronnie Cass, scriptwriter and musician, to make the final arrangements. Both Tom Jones and Ronnie Cass, (who said, 'You came, you sang, you conquered') were made Honorary Members of the choir.

Tom Jones and his 'Jones Choir': John Cynan Jones, Elwyn Jones, Kevin Jones, Islwyn Jones, Gwyn Jones, Will Jones, Bryn Jones, Tom Jones (accompanist), Tom Jones (chorister) and Eddie Jones. A great party followed in the BBC canteen with Lonnie Donegan, Dave Allen, Charlie Drake, Windsor Davies and Tom Jones leading the singing – although Tom was firmly told by manager Gordon Mills to keep quiet and save the voice! It was a late night – or rather an early morning, when choristers finally retired to their beds in London's Gower Street.

Filming the second Tom Jones Christmas show with Ella Fitzgerald, 30 November 1970. Earlier in the year the choir appeared on the Harry Secombe Show with Nina, Sacha Distel and Donald Houston, before accepting a second invitation to spend four days at Boreham Wood for another Tom Jones show. Despite being reprimanded by John Cynan for singing half a beat too slow, Ms Fitzgerald was so impressed with the choir that she dedicated her special arrangement of *Just A Closer Walk With Thee*, to them.

Five

The Crusaders
1971-1980

The singing of the Treorchy Male Choir can always be guaranteed to stir the emotions of all those who hear them. Long may this continue.

The Rt Hon Lord Callaghan of Cardiff

Filming the television programme *Sing Aloud* at the HTV Studios in Cardiff, 7 December 1975 with Wynford Vaughan Thomas and soprano Eirwen Jones. They also recorded a *Sound and Vision* TV show there, although this time under the direction of accompanist Jennifer Jones due to John Cynan's illness.

Treorchy Male Choir official photograph, Noddfa Chapel, Treorchy 1971. Owing to the death of accompanist Tom Jones in August 1971, Marion Williams became deputy accompanist for a short time before taking up a teaching post in Kent. The second choir accompanist was later announced as Jennifer Jones and her first concert was in St David's Cathedral where composer Mansel Thomas conducted the choir for the first performance of his arrangement of *Fantasia on Famous Welsh Hymn Tunes*.

Jennifer Jones, accompanist 1971-1988. Trained at the Royal Academy of Music, London she appeared as a performer on both the piano and the harp in concerts and commercial recordings with the choir. Her dedication and total commitment to the organization endeared her to all. As accompanist she undertook four overseas tours before her resignation in 1988. She is currently the conductor of the Ynysowen Male Voice Choir and still lives in Treorchy.

Filming the Burt Bacharach show with Tom Jones, February 1971. A group of choristers were invited to record the show at the ATV Studios, Borehamwood in a scene depicting a Welsh tavern at the turn of the century with the men wearing colliers' costumes. The show later won an Emmy Award in the USA and the choir received a special commendation at the ceremony for its performance. In December they made the third Tom Jones Christmas show.

Treorchy Male Choir and the Second Generation singing *O Come All Ye Faithful* with Julie Andrews on her Christmas show, 26 November 1973. Also on the show was Peggy Lee and Peter Ustinov and the choir performed a series of Christmas carols for the national broadcast. Free beer was served in the studio canteen on the final night and a huge party was held with Leslie Crowther, Glyn Houston and Sheila Sims in attendance.

Julie Andrews Christmas show line up, November 1973. The choir enjoyed an incredibly successful television career during the early 1970s, particularly with Tom Jones. They also sang with Iris Williams at a St David's Day concert in 1972 and on the 2,000th performance of *Good Morning Wales* with Ryan Davies and Max Boyce. Max said, 'My mam told me "now you've arrived, singing with Treorchy". And do you know? My mother's right.'

John Cynan Jones presenting Julie Andrews with a choir shield and the latest EMI recording in November 1973. The connection with the EMI record company had long since been established, with annual commercial recordings made at the Brangwyn Hall in Swansea. During the year they even recorded the Japanese national anthem, *Kimigayo* for background music to a Japanese rugby television programme.

Treorchy Male Choir official picture taken outside St Peter's church, Pentre, 14 July 1974. They later made the Ryan Davies TV show, dressed once more in miner's outfits in a scene filmed in Dumfries Street, Treorchy. In Llandrindod Wells the second tenors went down well as the stage collapsed beneath them and in November they made the Max Boyce Show with the Benny Litchfield Orchestra.

Choir chairman Bob Griffiths presenting treasurer Gwynne Williams, with an initialed brief case for meritorious service to the Treorchy Male Choir, outside St Peter's church, Pentre, 14 July 1974. A county councillor and JP, Gwynne joined the choir in 1948 and was its distinguished treasurer from 1951 until his death in 1980 when he was succeeded by publicity officer John Mallin, who has remained in the post ever since.

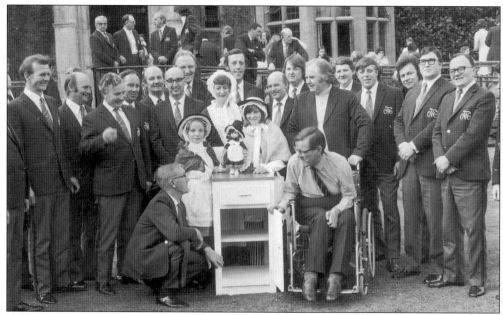

Presenting furniture to The Great House, Cheshire Home, Chippenham, 26 April 1975. The association between the choir and the home was nurtured by chairman of the branch, Reg Coates. In September, 1972 The Treorchy Male Choir Room was opened there and patients often visited the rehearsal room to strengthen the bond between both organizations. The choir also presented the home with bedside lockers and numerous commercial recordings over the years.

Enjoying a few drinks following a concert in 1976. During the year the choir undertook their longest distance travelled to a concert by coach when they sang in Hull City Hall. The choir is divided into two buses, one nicknamed The Deacons, because they travel straight home following a concert and the second called The Rodneys because they enjoy some 'liquid refreshment' in the nearest hostelry – purely medicinal purposes of course!

Filming the Sir Geraint Evans' Christmas show, *Celebrations*, 11 June 1977 at the HTV Studios, Cardiff, which was viewed by 180 TV companies worldwide and used to spearhead sales of Welsh programmes. The famous operatic baritone performed *Arglwydd Mae Yn Nosi* and the choir later rehearsed it as part of their repertoire. It is now performed as a mark of respect on the death of a choristers.

Torquay Central Church, 18 June 1977. Less than a year later the choir witnessed the final performance of prize-winning elocutionist Herbert Jones. He made 152 appearances over a ten year period with the choir, having already claimed 200 awards from eisteddfodau and appeared on stage at the Old Vic. Some of his most memorable monologues were *I Forget I Forget, The Barber Kept On Shaving* and *Jacob Strauss*.

Blenheim Palace, 24 May 1977. The choir made a television programme called *Airs and Graces* with the BBC Midland Radio Orchestra and The Settlers on the South Terrace of Vanburgh's masterpiece. The choir performed *Muss-I-den* and *Myfanwy* for the broadcast.

Blenheim Palace, 24 May 1977. From left to right: John Callaghan, Bob Griffiths, Will Jones, Gwyn Jones and Michael Gale. Later that year assistant accompanist Neil Johnson resigned from the position, less than two years after accepting it. The choir also joined forces with Harry Secombe on yet another of his popular TV shows.

Viscount Tonypandy George Thomas, the former Speaker of the House of Commons with chairman John Davies, vice chairman Danny Williams, conductor John Cynan Jones and secretary Donna Griffiths at the choir's Annual Dinner and Dance December 17, 1977 in the Connaught Rooms, Cardiff. 'Our George' remained a good friend for many years, writing the foreword for the choir's commemorative fiftieth anniversary publication in 1996.

Meeting HRH Princess Alexandria at the Rhondda Sports Centre, 27 April 1978. Her Royal Highness attended the performance, in aid of the Queen's Jubilee Appeal Fund, which also featured Patricia O'Neill and the Mid-Glamorgan Youth Brass Band, under the leadership of Ieuan Morgan. The Princess requested that the choir perform *Myfanwy*.

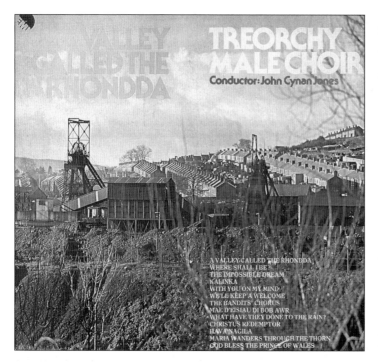

A *Valley Called The Rhondda* record sleeve. Under the guidance of John Cynan Jones, a pioneer in recognising the social upheaval of the 1960s and 1970s, the choir gradually moved into the unchartered territory of lighter music. The choir benefited enormously from the commissioned arrangements by Mike Sammes, starting with *Impossible Dream* which was used on this recording. It became obvious that Treorchy were the forerunners in this new field, allowing other male choirs to follow.

Dudley Town Hall, 18 November 1978. The artist for the evening was Wyn Davies who remained tenor soloist for more than fifteen years. Some of his most memorable songs, which were performed in concert and on many of the choir's albums, were *Three Bells (Jimmy Brown)*, *Kalinka*, *O Gymru*, *Smile Beyond The Looking Glass* and *Bring Him Home*.

Receiving a plaque from W.D. Jones on behalf of the Rhondda Recognition Committee for projecting the valley's musical life, Park and Dare Theatre, Treorchy, 30 November 1978. Earlier in the year the choir changed its uniform to dress suits and made a TV documentary on World Cup referee Clive Thomas whose father was a Life Member.

Treorchy Male Choir official picture, 1979. Earlier in the year they performed in the Ryan Davies Memorial Concert in the New Theatre, Cardiff with Harry Secombe, Delme Bryn Jones, Helen Field and Bryn Williams.

The choir's Annual Dinner and Dance with Lord Parry, chairman of the Welsh Tourist Board, Angel Hotel, Cardiff, May 1979. It was held in honour of Donna Griffiths who had retired as choir secretary after almost thirty years. Lord Parry said, 'The men of Treorchy Male Choir have become stars in themselves.'

Chorister Benny Griffiths and Ronnie Corbett on the set of an episode of 'The Worm That Turned' from *The Two Ronnies* show, Deep Navigation Colliery, Treharris, 9 August 1980. Suitably dressed in a miner's costume and having fun, often wondering who the comedians really were, Ronnie Barker asked the men to sing *In the Evening*. He later said, 'The choir is the best in choral singing. How can they be described except in superlatives? They are without equal.'

W.J. 'Donna' Griffiths retired as secretary after twenty-eight years faithful service and his successor was Islwyn Morgan. Islwyn joined the choir in 1947 and took up the post of assistant secretary in 1975, followed by secretary in 1980. A faithful and admirable servant to the choir, Islwyn retired from the post in 2001, having been responsible for more than 720 engagements, nine overseas tours, three conductors and three accompanists. His contribution to the choir has been truly magnificent.

Filming the TV show *Sing To The Lord* with the Welsh Brass Consort, Conway Road Methodist Church, Cardiff, 6 September 1980. For the next three years the choir benefited enormously from the services of talented soprano Josephine Jones who performed in twenty-nine concerts with them before emigrating to South Africa.

Travelling to Canada for the choir's first overseas tour in seventeen years on 19 October 1980. This picture was taken in Llantrisant before the choir headed off to Pirbright Army Barracks for a celebratory send off! Choristers stayed the night, travelling to the airport on the following morning to undertake the exhausting two week tour which included eleven sell out concert performances in Toronto, Barrie, Gravenhurst, Kapuskasing, Ottawa, Orillia, Elliot Lake and Niagra Falls.

Visiting Niagra Falls, Canada, October 1980. During the two week tour the choir travelled 2,200 miles by road and performed for more than 8,000 people. The soloists for the duration of the tour were Sam Griffiths, Wyn Davies and bass Harry Price, 'the singing dustman', best known for his spine-tingling performance of *Just a Closer Walk* and regular cast member of TWW's programme *Gwlad Y Gan (Land of Song)* with Ivor Emmanuel.

Six

Music of the Night
1981-1990

As a Welshman who can't sing, I never feel more proud to be Welsh than when I hear the Treorchy Male Choir – the master choir of them all. If I could sing, I would apply for membership myself.

Sir Anthony Hopkins

On stage at the Sydney Opera House, 14 October 1986. Treorchy Male Choir was the first Welsh choir to perform there. The concert was sold out weeks in advance and a second concert was called for within three days – this was also a sell out engagement.

81

Baritone soloist Sam Griffiths was presented with an Italian crystal decanter and glasses from choir president Cliff Taylor, 7 July 1981. This presentation was to mark his 250th concert performance. He retired from public performance due to ill health in 1988, after more than forty years of faithful service to the choir.

The dedication of a display cabinet in memory of Tom Jones (accompanist), Donna Griffiths (secretary) and Gwynne Williams (treasurer), rehearsal room, 18 September 1981. From left to right: John Cynan Jones (conductor), John Haydn Davies (conductor emeritus), school teacher Meurig Hughes (later choir chairman) who helped with the construction of the cabinet, Cliff Taylor (president), Islwyn Morgan (secretary).

Strasbourg, France, 25 September 1981. Although fraught with administrative difficulties, the highlight of the visit was the performance in the Roman Catholic High Mass at Strasbourg Cathedral. The most awe-inspiring moment was the final section of *Tydi a Roddaist*, allowing the celebrant to comment, 'Thanks to the choir of Treorchy, who have sung their songs in a manner worthy of this building.'

Strasbourg, France, 25 September 1981. The choir undertook a three day tour of Strasbourg and appeared in the magnificent cathedral before a congregation of almost 4,000 people. The first concert in the Kungress Hall was broadcast on French radio and on the following evening the choir performed in the Palais des Fêtes. From left to right: Alun Dawies, Mal Johnson, Daryl Stacey, Peter Jones, Michael Peachey.

Bryn Yemm and the choir promoting their joint album, *How Great Thou Art*, 1982. There was a busy time ahead as the choir gave a private concert for 100 supporters and members of the New Zealand Rugby Team and made a second album within two weeks. Later in the year they gave three performances in Nottingham – the first was to honour Harry Mortimer on his eightieth birthday and on the last visit the choir was actually flown there from Cardiff! On 18 September they became the first choir to perform in the new St David's Hall, Cardiff.

Sir Geraint Evans joining choristers and wives at the Annual Dinner and Dance, Seabank Hotel, Porthcawl, 1984. During the previous year the choir made the Leo Sayer Show with Richard Clayderman, performed in Eton College with Dickie Henderson and later in a TV programme with Harry Secombe. The national press stated, 'Treorchy is the Welsh male choir that others try to imitate' and were later named as one of the top three choirs in the world by a BBC survey.

Management Committee, Treorchy Male Choir 1984-1985. In September 1983 they backed Tom Jones for a performance of *Green Green Grass of Home* to mark his new UK tour. The *Western Mail* pointed out, 'It was probably the best backing group he has ever had.' During the following month the choir performed in a gala concert to honour Viscount Tonpandy with Glyn and Donald Houston, Dewi Griffiths, Pendyrus Male Choir, Cory Band and Cliff Morgan at Rhondda Sports Centre.

Nuclear Plant, Deep River, Canada, 25 October 1985. Thanks to Honorary Member Harold Woody, the choir undertook an eight-concert tour of Canada, with the most memorable performance before a capacity crowd in the magnificent Roy Thomson Hall, Toronto. With an extraordinary 'Last Night Of The Proms' atmosphere, coupled with the choir's outstanding singing and John Cynan's typically professional showmanship, the concert is ranked as one of the greatest in the history of the Treorchy Male Choir.

Preparing to walk under Niagra Falls, Ontario, Canada, October 1985. The choir also appeared in Gravenhurst, Deep River, Kingston, Montreal, Pembroke and Niagra Falls, where they took full advantage of sightseeing one of the wonders of the world.

Canada, October 1985. The tour also included an extra addition to the music staff, in deputy conductor John Beddoe, who later left to take up the baton as musical director of the Llantrisant Male Choir. During the trip to Kingston, the choir's bus driver Bob Merrill was taken to hospital. In a typically good-hearted gesture, the choir visited his ward and sang *Myfanwy* around the bed, much to the surprize of the medical staff and patients alike!

Canada, 1985. The choir was delighted when soprano Mair Roberts, the conductor of Cantorion Creigiau, joined them on the tour. Earlier in the year they made a Christmas record single in the Wembley CPS Studio with Patty Boulaye, although it was never released because a rival recorded the same song shortly afterwards. Ms Boulaye said, 'Treorchy are brilliant and what a privilege it is to have worked with them. They certainly created the heavenly atmosphere we needed for the recording'.

Treorchy Male Choir official picture, 1985. That year the choir appeared in the *Songs of Praise* TV show and performed in the Opera House, Blackpool with Ken Dodd. Following the concert they marched across the stage and gave a second performance in the nearby Winter Gardens Ballroom. Later in the year they appeared for the first time in the York Festival and sang for Diana, Princess of Wales at the official opening of the Callord and Bowser sweet factory in Bridgend.

The choir performing in the school room under the baton of bandmaster Ieuan Morgan for a promotional video recording made in preparation for the Australian Tour, 4 January 1986. A heavy snowfall meant that neither John Cynan Jones nor Jennifer Jones could attend rehearsals. Actor Anthony Hopkins appeared on a *Desert Island Discs* show and of his eight choices, chose two of the choir's recordings of *Myfanwy* and *Hen Wlad Fy Nhadau*.

Performing at Wiggins Teep, in the presence of HRH Princess Anne to mark the official opening of the £15 million paper mill, Cardiff, 5 June 1986. The invitation came thanks to a suggestion by one of the choristers who worked there. At the Park and Dare Annual Concert, baritone Derek Walker joined 104 choristers on stage – the largest performing choir since 1963.

Choristers Mike Gale, Eddie 'Ike' Evans, Reg Stephens, Islwyn Morgan, Roger Morse and Bryn Howells filming the *Corau Mawr* television show in The New Inn, Ton Pentre, 24 June 1986. Made by production company Scan for S4C, the hour-long programme was based solely on Treorchy and featured interviews from the music staff, choristers plus an outstanding performance of Mike Sammes' new arrangement of *My Way* – complete with lightning bolt for special effect!

Giving a pre-concert performance at Milton Keynes Rugby Club, 28 June 1986. The rather long afternoon was so memorable that every chorister was given honorary membership of the club! It could have been a lot longer if bus steward Benny Griffiths, the man with a thousands hilarious sayings, hadn't got typically lost getting there!

Victoria Methodist Church, Weston-super-Mare, 5 July 1986. This concert was filmed for Australian TV and also marked Sam Griffiths' last engagement as choir soloist. During Jennifer's short illness, Jane Gordon became accompanist.

Preparing to board the coaches outside Treorchy post office, before heading for the airport and flying to Sydney to begin their legendary three-week tour of Australia, 10 October 1986. They were invited on this special trip by the James Hardie Industries to commemorate the 150th anniversary of South Australia. No other choir had ever been invited to undertake such a high-profile tour.

Ken Simcox, Reg Stephens, Roy Bobbett, Bryn Howells, Peter Jones, Arwel Evans and Phil Edmunds on Sydney Harbour, 13 October 1986. During the three week trip, the choir performed for tens of thousands of people and travelled thousands of miles, enjoying celebrity status throughout the country with regular TV and radio appearances.

Kevin Davies, Daryl Stacey, Mike Jones, Gary Williams, Bert John, Bob Griffiths, Reg Stephens, Jack Bean, Phil Edmunds, Dave Phillips, Peter Jones and Bryn Howells relaxing on board the choir's private yacht, the *Matilda* in Sydney Harbour, October 1986. The bucks fizz was a firm favourite as choristers viewed the awesome surroundings in total disbelief. As chorister (and future chairman) Roger Morse exclaimed, 'They made me feel like a millionaire.'

JAMES HARDIE INDUSTRIES LIMITED

presents
the internationally acclaimed

TREORCHY MALE CHOIR

on their first Australian tour

SYDNEY	NEWCASTLE	WHYALLA	PORT PIRIE	RENMARK	MT GAMBIER	ADELAIDE	MELBOURNE
Sydney Opera House	Civic Theatre	Middleback Theatre	Keith Michell Theatre	Chaffey Theatre	Sir Robert Helpmann Theatre	Festival Theatre	Victorian Arts Centre
Oct 14 and 17	Oct 15	Oct 19	Oct 20	Oct 21	Oct 23	Oct 27	Oct 29 and 30

Watch local press for booking details

Australian tour poster, 1986. During the three-week fully sponsored trip they performed fourteen concerts throughout the southern states, with venues including Whyalla, Renmark, Mount Gambier, Newcastle, Melbourne's Victoria Arts Centre and twice in the magnificent Sydney Opera House and Adelaide Festival Theatre because of increased demand for tickets. Each concert was rewarded with a magnificent standing ovation.

Choristers enjoying the sunshine on Bondi Beach, Sydney, Australia, October 1986. Two choristers will always be remembered for their attire on the sands – braces, jackets and knotted handkerchiefs! While one chorister will never forget his dive into the sea in Newcastle when the wave suddenly disappeared and he landed face-first in the sand.

On the steps of the Sydney Opera House, Australia, 14 October 1986. They performed before two consecutive packed houses at the Opera House. From the outset of *Cwm Rhondda*, the success of the night was ensured as thousands of admirers, many sitting outside the auditorium and listening to loud speakers, were totally overcome by the magnificent performance. The Australian press said, 'Sing their hearts out at the Opera House they did, and proved once again that the Treorchy Male Choir is one of the great choirs of the world.'

The choir's first engagement on the Australian tour was in St Martin's Place Amphitheatre, Sydney, 14 October 1986. Tour organizers John Reid, Doug Firstbrook, Brian Anstee and James Kelso were all made Honorary Members of the choir and James Hardie Industries press officer Linde McPherson was presented with a choir plaque in recognition of their hard work in ensuring its success.

Sydney, Australia, October 1986. John Cynan Jones and the choir worked tirelessly in preparation for the tour 'down under'. The conductor joined accomplished pianist Brian Davies to compose a choral arrangement of the Australian folk song *Click Go The Shears,* and John Cynan kindly reminded the audience to listen to the special piano sequences because 'the jokes are over there...!'

Choristers backstage at the Melbourne Victoria Arts Centre, Australia, 29 October 1986. The choir gave two concerts in the theatre before packed audiences of more than 2,600 people. John Cynan's repertoire on stage received plenty of acclaim, particularly when translating the Welsh words of *Harlech* as he described the scene of carnage and blood dripping off the swords. 'English blood of course,' he would exclaim.

Treorchy Male Choir's 40th Anniversary Dinner and Dance, Seabank Hotel, Porthcawl, 1986. From left to right: John Mallin, Islwyn Morgan, Mayor John Davies, Bob Griffiths, broadcaster Alun Williams and Rhondda MP Alan Rogers.

Sir Harry Secombe's 40th Anniversary in Showbusiness Dinner, Grosvenor House, London, 14 November 1986. A selected number of choristers were invited to perform in this glittering event. The choir sang *My Way*, receiving a thunderous standing ovation from the capacity audience.

Sir Harry Secombe's 40th Anniversary in Showbusiness Dinner. The celebrity audience included Lulu, Ron Moody, Leslie Crowther, The Beverly Sisters, Barry Cryer, Jimmy Tarbuck, Sir Geraint Evans, Viscount Tonypandy and Angela Rippon. The gripping climax was a joint performance between Sir Harry and the choir of *We'll Keep A Welcome*.

The choir with Viscount Tonypandy George Thomas and Tom Jones during the filming of *Born to Be Me*, St David's Hall, Cardiff, November 1987. The choir spent a week filming the programme, which marked their sixth project with the singer. Produced by Ronnie Cass, the choir sang in St David's Hall, at the Culverhouse Cross HTV studios and at a Cardiff pub.

Civic Reception at Warrington Town Hall, prior to the choir's performance at the nearby Parr Hall organized by Life Member Mel Absolam, 14 November 1987. The choir later performed for Diana, Princess of Wales at St David's Hall, and helped to raise £15,000 for Barnados. Later in the year they appeared in a Variety Club of Great Britain ceremony in City Hall, Cardiff as a tribute to Rhondda-born sportsman and personality Cliff Morgan.

Taken from the record sleeve cover of the *Together* recording with Sir Harry Secombe, 1987. The choir made the album at their favourite recording venue, Brangwyn Hall, Swansea, while Sir Harry's voice was dubbed onto it much later. The choir made the TV programme *Myfanwy*, walking the length of Dumfries Street, Treorchy. It was a memorable event for one particular chorister whose single tear rolling down the cheek was filmed up-close to add to the poignant affect of the Welsh love song!

Dudley Town Hall, 20 February 1988. Jennifer Jones conducted the choir at this event due to John Cynan Jones' illness. Fun-loving Jennifer and pianist Brian Davies once wore Indian head-dress to perform *Crossing the Plains*. In October the choir performed the first of three Christie Tyler Furniture Fortnight concerts at the invitation of Nigel Phillips. Each year the choir gave ten consecutive after-dinner concerts at the City Hall, Cardiff along with such performers as Mike Doyle, George Melly and Ray Allan (with Lord Charles of course!)

Cliff Morgan's *This is Your Life* TV programme with Nerys Hughes, Glenys and Neil Kinnock and Harry Carpenter, 7 December 1988. The choir filmed the surprise show, hosted by Michael Aspel at the Teddington Studios in London. Also present were a host of sports personalities and celebrities, including Des Lynam, Gloria Hunniford and Sir Geraint Evans.

Choir publicity officer John Davies and Labour Leader Neil Kinnock following the filming of *This is Your Life* at the Teddington Studios, London 7 December 1988. Mr Kinnock, Owain Arwel Hughes and Cliff Morgan all 'auditioned' for the part of conductor during the festivities and Sir Alastair Burnett later wrote a letter to Treorchy, explaining, 'This is your life Treorchy would take up a whole evening's television to do you justice.'

Angela Rippon and choristers at George Thomas' 80th Birthday Concert, St David's Hall, Cardiff, 29 January 1989. The choir shared the stage with Penelope Keith, Siân Philips, Stuart Burrows and the Band of the Welsh Guards.

Marion Williams, accompanist 1989-1998. On becoming the full-time accompanist, Marion came 'home' after eighteen years, she had previously accompanied the choir's victorious performance at the National Eisteddfod, Bala in 1967. Whilst still at school she became a part-time student at the Welsh College of Music and Drama and gained many prizes, before being awarded two diplomas. She then went to Goldsmiths' College, London where she gained a Bachelor of Music. After taking up a teaching post in Sevenoaks, Kent in 1971, she then taught in Oxford before returning to South Wales to settle in Barry.

Pirbright Army Barracks, 1989. Since the re-formation of the choir, members have always enjoyed a good relationship with the armed forces. Over the years they have been guests at the Sergeants' Messes of many army barracks throughout the country, including Pirbright, Cosford and Sandhurst. But probably the best friendship was forged with officials at RAF Lyneham, where choristers often stop for refreshments on the way home from nearby concerts or following a lengthy international rugby weekend at Twickenham!

Meeting Her Majesty Queen Elizabeth II at Powys Castle, 21 April 1989. The choir was invited to perform in a pageant celebrating the 300th anniversary of the Royal Welch Fusiliers. During the concert they were asked to sing *Happy Birthday* to Her Majesty and tenor Wyn Davies gave a memorable performance of *Dafydd y Garreg Wen* next to the tableau illuminating the carnage at the Battle of the Somme. It was also an unforgettable overnight visit due to the poor state of accommodation offered to the choristers!

Cory Band Fire Benevolent Fund Concert, St David's Hall, 9 July 1990. Earlier that year the choir performed a celebrity concert in St David's Hall, with baritone Donald Maxwell, but the buses were delayed because the Cory Band rehearsal room had been devastated by fire. In an effort to raise money for the appeal fund, the choir later performed with the band at the capital city venue.

Cory Band Fire Benevolent Fund Concert, St David's Hall, Cardiff, 9 July 1990. During the year the choir made its first album on the new CD format and performed its seventh concert at the popular Fairfield Hall, Croydon. Organized by former EMI producer Bob Barratt, the sell-out concert was often attended by Treorchy's commissioned arranger, musician Mike Sammes.

Seven

My Way
1991-2000

Their work brings honour not only to themselves and Treorchy, but to their country.

Dennis O'Neill

Australian Tour Publicity Picture, October 1999. Between 1990 and 2000, the choir undertook five highly successful overseas tours. They included four trips to the United States of America, with one incorporating Canada. During the visits they performed in California, Colorado, Georgia, Nebraska, Minnesota, Iowa, Oregon and Washington. In November 1999, they performed twenty-two engagements on a month-long sell out tour of Australia.

Highway TV programme, 6 February 1991. For the first time in the history of the popular television series, it dedicated its thirty-minute slot to an organization rather than a particular place. The choir spent three very enjoyable days filming and recording with Sir Harry Secombe and Cliff Morgan.

Sir Harry Secombe acting 'The Goon' at the Park and Dare Theatre, Treorchy, during the filming of Highway, 6 February 1991. The choir recorded the programme from HTV Culverhouse Cross Studios, Park and Dare Theatre, St Peter's church and at the rehearsal room. John Cynan Jones, Marion Williams, John Davies, publicity officer and chorister Norman Cox were interviewed on the show.

On song with Sir Harry Secombe, Highway, 6 February 1991. Part of the programme was dedicated to interviewing three very good friends of the choir – Honorary Member Brian Bates, Adrian Dix and his wife, Val. For many years the three individuals, who live in Cheltenham, followed the choir to every venue throughout the UK. Brian has also raised tens of thousands of pounds for the choir and for charities by organizing concerts with the help of his friends, Judy and Nigel Chivers.

John Cynan Jones conducting at a Christie Tyler event in the City Hall, Cardiff, February 1991. In April the choir joined forces with Pontarddulais and Morriston Orpheus Male Choirs and the Band of the Welsh Guards to record EMI's *Christmas From The Land Of Song*. The disc was so successful that it received a Silver Disc Award for 60,000 copies sold. To date Treorchy has made almost fifty albums and singles, making them arguably the most recorded male choir in the world.

John Cynan Jones' last concert as conductor in the Borough Theatre, Abergavenny, 27 April 1991. This was probably the most difficult year in the re-formed history of the choir. After twenty-two years as musical director, during which time he conducted more than 650 concerts, four tours and radically lead the choir into the realm of light music, John Cynan Jones retired due to ill health, just months prior to the choir's first US tour. Within weeks of his resignation the choir was given the saddest of news with the death of their founder conductor, John Haydn Davies.

John Jenkins, conductor 1991-1997. Born in Neath, he read music at University College of Cardiff and London University. He gained performance and teaching diplomas at the Welsh College of Music and Drama and the Royal College of Music and in 1974 was appointed Music Adviser to the West Glamorgan County Council. His work in establishing orchestras, choirs and bands led to three Prince of Wales Awards for music excellence and was a recipient of the Guild of the Promotion of Welsh Music. Under his direction the choir reached new musical heights, performing such magnificent works as the *Kullervo Symphony* and Beethoven's *Choral Fantasia*, while also recording the critically acclaimed album devoted to music by rock band Queen.

The Late Bus – or The Rodneys – during the tour of the American Midwest, October 1991. The two-week tour was a thoroughly enjoyable, if exhausting experience, with the choir performing fifteen concerts and travelling thousands of miles by coach. During the visit they toured Nebraska, Minnesota and Iowa before flying to Washington D.C.

Seventh Day Adventist Church, Lincoln, Nebraska, 27 October 1991. Organized by Fran and George Wheat, the choir entertained packed houses in some of the largest concert halls and cathedrals in the Midwest. Under the baton of their new conductor, who had only weeks to rehearse, the tour was a great success. Despite spending hours each day on the coaches, rushing to the hotel rooms, changing, performing and then enjoying some midnight fun in the bar, the choristers battled exhaustion to make this a successful trip – revelling in the camaraderie and fun-loving attitude of their fellow members.

Teikyo University, Nebraska, October 1991. During the long hours of travel across the flat lands of the Midwest, choristers enjoyed a wonderful visit to Boystown, where they gave an unforgettable performance for the talented choir of young orphaned children. They also spent time on a Indian Reservation where they were treated to the ritualistic dancing of the Native American Sioux.

Capitol Certificate, Washington DC, 1991. To commemorate the choir's tour of the Midwest and Washington DC, two US flags were flown above the Capitol. The first was in recognition of the choir and the second was a gift to retiring conductor John Cynan Jones who had always hoped to tour the country himself. He was later awarded the position of conductor Emeritus of the Treorchy Male Choir.

Author Dean Powell with friends Alwyn Lewis and Bryn Howells, Washington DC, 1 November 1991. The tour was completed with a weekend of sightseeing in the nation's capital, along with a final performance in Baltimore, Maryland. As far as the choristers were concerned it was the highlight of the trip, giving them the opportunity to visit the White House, US Capitol, Lincoln Memorial, Jefferson Memorial, Vietnam War Memorial and the grave-side of John F. Kennedy at Arlington Cemetery.

Choristers enjoying a rugby international weekend at St Andrews Golf Club, Scotland, February 1992. Later they recorded the soundtrack by composer Trevor Herbert for an animated version of Dylan Thomas' *Under Milk Wood* in the BBC Swansea studio where the poet often broadcast. Actor Brian Blessed also visited the rehearsal room to record his radio programme and said, 'The power and dignity you express in your singing conveys completely the unbeatable fiery spirit of the Welsh people.'

Rehearsing with the Royal Philharmonic Orchestra and Owain Arwel Hughes at the Henry Wood Hall, London, 19 July 1992. A few days later Treorchy became the first British choir to perform Sibelius' complex *Kullervo Symphony* in Finnish. This incredible undertaking earned the choir great respect from classical musicians the world over, following an outstanding televised performance accompanied by soloists Jason Howard and Helen Field at St David's Hall, Cardiff as part of the Welsh Proms.

Filming the Roy Noble TV programme *On Mortality*, Treorchy Cemetery, December 1992. The year was also significant because the choir joined 8,000 other male voices in the first World Choir concert in Cardiff Arms Park with Dennis O'Neill, Tom Jones and Dame Gwyneth Jones, under the guidance of Owain Arwel Hughes. The choir also performed on Brighton Racecourse and for foreign ambassadors at the Grosvenor House Hotel, London.

Peachtree Shopping Mall, Atlanta, Georgia, USA, 10 February 1993. At the invitation of the World Choir organization, the choir undertook a five-day tour of Atlanta to help promote a possible massed choral concert in the city during the following year. They gave twelve performances in such unlikely venues as office blocks, shopping malls, hotels and at the magnificent Atlanta Dome football stadium.

Ben Hill Methodist Church, Atlanta, Georgia, USA, 10 February 1993. which was probably the most emotional performance by the choir for an all-black congregation at their church. Such was the intensity of their religious faith that the singing of hymns and spiritual items, especially *Were You There*, brought the congregation to its knees. It was an unforgettable occasion, with choir chairman John Davies, who died only months later, giving one of his most memorable speeches in his own inimitable manner. The choir later linked hands with members of the congregation for a joint performance of *Jacob's Ladder*.

Performing before the crypt and eternal flame of Dr Martin Luther King Jr, Atlanta, Georgia, USA, 9 February 1993. Treorchy became the first white choir to perform on an all-black network television show, entitled The Bobby Jones Gospel Explosion. During the visit they also toured the headquarters of the Coca Cola Company and performed for students and lecturers at the University of Georgia Music Department.

Conductor John Jenkins, international baritone Jason Howard and choir chairman John Davies with representatives of Barclays Bank who sponsored the choir's performance of Beethoven's *Choral Fantasia* at St David's Hall, Cardiff, 2 April 1993. During the year the choir made a demo-recording for the World Choir concert which featured Shirley Bassey and performed on the *Good Morning* TV show.

Abbey Road Studios, London, 26 June 1993. After months of painstaking preparation the choir's most ambitious recording was made in the same studio once used by The Beatles. *Treorchy Sing Queen* was an EMI album of music by Freddie Mercury and also featured members of 10cc and vocalist Carl Wayne. Fully exploring the amazing versatility of the choir, the album was a great success and earned the admiration of Queen band member Brian May who wrote a glowing letter of appreciation to them.

Treorchy Male Choir official photograph, October 1993. Months later, the choir was saddened with the news of the death of broadcaster Alun Williams who had been such a close friend for so many years and were proud to perform in his Memorial Concert at St David's Hall with Jeff Hooper, Dewi Griffiths, Cliff Morgan and Max Boyce on 27 March 1994.

Songs of Praise, Penrhys, Rhondda, 3 October 1993. During the two-day recording they were filmed from a helicopter performing *A Valley Called The Rhondda* at the amphitheatre, Penrhys. They also spent a day in the Park and Dare Theatre, under the direction of conductor Dr Terry James for a massed male choir concert. Only months later they broadcast *We Are The Champions* from the same venue as part of the Roy Noble programme, *On The Noble Trail*.

Opening ceremony of Highway 85, California, USA, 15 October 1994. Dubbed the 'Treorchy Mile', the choir was one of many musical organizations taking part in the official opening before more than 20,000 people. The two-week sell out tour of California and Colorado was a magnificent event, organized by Marge and Ed Fraser of Sunnyvale. It was on this tour that the Clec Committee was formed – four choristers gathering daily to discuss idiotic mistakes made by fellow singers and then holding an award ceremony on board the coaches pointing out the mishaps!

Alcatraz, San Francisco, California, USA, 16 October 1994. With so much free time on their hands, the choristers enjoyed some wonderful sightseeing opportunities, not least of which was a trip over the Bay to Alcatraz Island. Later in the day they gave an outstanding concert in the magnificent Grace Cathedral on Nob Hill, for a capacity audience, made all the more memorable by its incredible – and particularly daunting – acoustics!

Yosemite National Park, California, USA, 20 October 1994. Probably the highlight of the tour was the two-night 'rest' at the magnificent Yosemite National Park. Fully appreciating the totally awesome surroundings of lush green forests and inspiring snow-capped peaks, choristers will never forget the sight of such a landscape.

Performing for Oscar-winning actress Joan Fontaine at the Penny Farthing Tavern, Salinas, California, USA, 23 October 1994. The legendary Hollywood film star of *Rebecca*, *Suspicion* and *Jane Eyre*, attended the choir's performance in Hartnell College, Salinas and was so impressed, she dined with them as part of her birthday celebrations. Ms Fontaine remained a firm admirer of the choir and kept in touch with author Dean Powell who also visited her Carmel home. She said 'No birthday was ever so memorable, you are all wonderful, thank you so much.'

Conductor John Jenkins with Honorary Member Evan James, Nevada City, California, 18 October 1994. For more than fifteen years Mr James, the descendant of the composers of *Hen Wlad Fy Nhadau*, the Welsh National Anthem, was one of the choir's major benefactors. A self-made millionaire who lived in Rolling Hills, California, he attended the choir's performance at Nevada City, where he also owned a ranch. Mr James passed away in March 2000.

On the steps of the USA Airforce Academy Chapel, Colorado Springs, Colorado, USA, 21 October 1994. For the final part of the tour the choir flew to Colorado and performed in Denver and Colorado Springs, again for capacity audiences, who typically rewarded them with standing ovations.

Walsall Town Hall, 13 May 1995. This performance was organized by long-standing supporter John Tucker. A few weeks later members of the choir performed on Queen Street bandstand, Cardiff for an audience of 4,000 people as the official welcoming party of world-famous American rock band, Bon Jovi. The choir also welcomed a new assistant accompanist in Heather James, who remained in the post for more than three years.

Choristers with wartime sweetheart Dame Vera Lynn, prior to her final official engagement before retirement, at her home village of Ditchling, Sussex, 28 May 1995. The performance was to mark the fiftieth anniversary since VE Day. Earlier in the year the choir was invited to perform before a packed congregation which included Lord Callaghan, at Llandaff Cathedral for the Memorial Service of their dear friend, Sir Cennydd Traherne, the Lord Lieutenant of Glamorgan, who said, 'The name of the village has surely been made famous by this great Treorchy Choir.'

Conductor John Jenkins launching the EMI recording, *Fifty Golden Years of Song* CD, November 1995. The choir's golden jubilee was a cause for great celebration and during the year they broadcast *Friday Night is Music Night* with Beverley Humphreys and Jason Howard and performed with the Halle Orchestra under the baton of Owain Arwel Hughes at the tenth anniversary of the Welsh Proms.

Haydn Erasmus and Cliburn Willis receiving commemorative watches as the two remaining founder members of the choir, Park and Dare Theatre, Treorchy, 10 October 1996. The choir gave three outstanding anniversary concerts during their fiftieth year, including a performance in the Brangwyn Hall, Swansea with Jason Howard, Ros Evans and Roy Noble and also produced a commemorative CD, plate, and publication.

A fiftieth anniversary reception at the Rhondda Cynon Taff Council Mayor's Parlour, January 1997. This reception took place just weeks after making a Christmas radio broadcast from Cardiff Castle with Max Boyce, Su Pollard and Don Maclean. Sadly, conductor John Jenkins was soon forced to resign due to ill health. Distinguished musician Alun John took control of the choir while a new conductor could be found. Treorchy's former deputy conductor, Andrew Badham, the musical director of Cwmbach Male Choir, accepted the position.

Andrew Badham, conductor since 1997. He studied the organ at the Welsh College of Music and Drama in Cardiff and choral conducting with Hungarian-born Celia Vadja, a former pupil of the famous composer Kodaly. Andrew went on to Phillipa Fawcett College, London, where he gained a teaching diploma. On leaving college he entered the Civil Service, working in the Department of Employment in Brixton, South London. Whilst there he was, for a period of time, organist and choirmaster at Holy Trinity Church, Upper Tooting. After returning to Wales he served as the conductor of the Mountain Ash Choral Society and the Cwmbach Male Choir. His first appointment as the new Musical Director for Treorchy was in a private dinner for the Lord Mayor of London at the Mansion House and he has since led them on two successful overseas tours.

The Centrum, Enchantment of Seas, 12 July 1997. Choristers were invited to perform at the official naming ceremony of the luxurious $3.2 billion Royal Caribbean cruise liner, Enchantment of the Seas. The choir sang in the vessel's Centrum and on Southampton Dock as the ship was officially named before an evening performance in the Carousel Lounge as the overnight cruise of the English Channel began.

Enchantment of Seas, Southampton, 12 July 1997. Treated as VIPs, the choir enjoyed a wonderful time on board the luxury liner with specially invited guests of the company. Following their final performance they were treated to a private concert by singer Petula Clark who wrote to them to express her admiration for their singing.

Enchantment of Seas, 12 July 1997. Although unenthusiastic to leave the opulence of the ship, the choir were treated to a very enjoyable afternoon – and evening – at their favourite watering hole, RAF Lyneham, on the way back to Wales. It was with the deepest regret, however, that the choir was later informed of the retirement of accompanist Marion Williams and associate accompanist Heather James.

Rehearsals for the Fiftieth Anniversary Concert, Treorchy Comprehensive School, October, 1997. Later that year the choir undertook a successful tour of Stockport, Carlisle and Halifax, where they performed with the Brighouse and Rastrick Brass Band, thanks to the hard work of Honorary Member Brian Bates and choir follower Harry Errington, and they appeared on stage with Jimmy Tarbuck at the Peugeot Car Company conference in Harrogate.

Fiftieth Anniversary Concert, St David's Hall, Cardiff, 28 November 1997. To conclude the choir's golden jubilee they gave an unforgettable concert with Dennis O'Neill and Rebecca Evans as soloists. The capacity audience, which included tenor Stuart Burrows, fully displayed their admiration for the choir's marvellous performance which stood as a testimony to their continued success as one of the world's finest musical organizations.

Rhiannon Williams, accompanist since 1998. She studied singing, piano, violin and harp from the age of eight. She won over ninety vocal competitions including the prestigious National BET Choirgirl of the Year Competition and made a number of solo appearances in the Royal Albert Hall, London. Her other achievements include membership of the National Youth Choir of Wales, National Youth Choir of Great Britain, Choir of St John's Smith Square and the Midlands and South West Cathedral Singers, with solo vocal parts being undertaken with the Mid Wales Centre for Opera at the young age of twelve. Awarded the Dorothy Atkinson Memorial Prize and the Henry, Edith and Constance Haddon Memorial Prize for piano, she received a part-time scholarship at the Royal Academy of Music and was musical director of the Anwen Little Theatre and official accompanist of Texaco Young Musician of the Year Competition.

Brian Bates, president since 1998. Although born in Narberth, West Wales, he settled in Cheltenham where he ran his own interior decorating business. He first heard the choir perform live in 1971 and has since travelled extensively to concerts and overseas tours. A devoted concert organizer, one of his first was in the Little Cottage Hospital in Burton-on-the-Water where his wife, Marion was being cared for but sadly died just days later. In 1983 he was recognized for his outstanding efforts by being awarded Honorary Membership and choristers remain indebted to him for his massive contribution organizing many fundraising concerts in aid of the choir.

Treorchy Male Choir official picture, May 1998. During the following year they made a Mike Brogdanov feature film, *A Light In The Valley* with Glyn Houston, which was filmed on the side of a very wet and windy Bwlch Mountain! Registered membership of the choir remains in excess of 115 choristers, the majority of whom live in a three mile radius of Treorchy. With two rehearsals a week, the choir undertakes more than thirty engagements per year, with the majority of them in aid of charity.

Royal Naval Academy Chapel, Greenwich, 15 May 1998. Due to the unavailability of Andrew Badham, conductor emeritus John Cynan Jones returned to the podium for the first time in eight years to conduct this very special concert for the Duke of Edinburgh Award Scheme. The 300 guests, led by Admiral Michael Gretton, paid £150 each for the private engagement which was a tremendous success.

Reunion Dinner of the 1974 British Lions Team, Cardiff Castle, 20 May 1999. The choir gave their debut public performance of the Bob Marley classic, *Stir It Up*, for British Rugby Charity, Woodenspoon. Earlier in the year they recorded the song on CD to raise funds for underprivileged children. It was officially launched on the opening day of the Rugby World Cup at the magnificent Millennium Stadium and the choir performed it again with group Ladysmith Black Mombazo at the Angel Hotel, Cardiff.

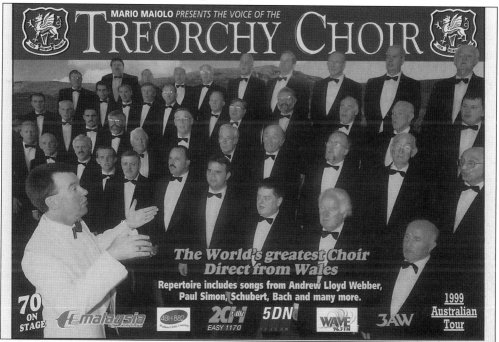

Australia Tour publicity poster, November 1999. Following an invitation by agent Mario Maiolo, the choir made a brilliant return tour of Australia, performing twenty-two engagements in twenty-eight days in some of the country's most magnificent venues. Following a week-long stay in Sydney, where the choir performed in the State Theatre, Newcastle's Civic Theatre, Wollongong (the choir's 1,500th performance since 1946) and later Armidale, they moved further east along the coast.

Surfer's Paradise, Gold Coast, Queensland, Australia, 12 November 1999. Following a performance in Lismore Town Hall, the choir followed the beautiful coastal road to their own private island, The Isle of Palms, for a relaxing weekend. Staying in individual homes, the choristers enjoyed all the facilities offered on the Gold Coast with sightseeing trips to local beaches or just relaxation in their private pool!

Queensland Performing Arts Centre, Brisbane, Australia, 12 November 1999. Probably one of the most truly awesome performances of the tour was for the 2,500 capacity audience in Brisbane. Waving Welsh flags, cheering and singing with the choir, this truly emotional performance will live long in the memory. The choir continued the tour with concerts in Coffs Harbour, Gosford, Canberra, Albury, Shepparton, Frankston, Morwell and in the beautiful Melbourne Regent Theatre before reaching Mount Gambier in South Australia.

Parliament Building, Adelaide, South Australia, 26 November 1999. This unforgettable tour reached its gripping climax in a weekend visit to Adelaide where they performed on the Friday evening before a 2,300 capacity audience in the great Performing Arts Centre. Another sell out concert took place in Tanunda on the following afternoon before a return, by popular demand, to Adelaide for a second concert in the Arts Centre. At the end-of-tour party choristers rejoiced in the success of a tour where they performed for well over 20,000 people.

Seattle, Washington, USA, 26 September 2000. Following an invitation by Honorary Member Ed Fraser, the choir undertook a two-week tour of Canada and the USA, with nine engagements along the west coast of the continent. Opening in Vancouver, British Columbia, they spent a long weekend in the affluent surroundings of Victoria on Vancouver Island, before crossing the water into the US city of Seattle and performing in venues throughout Washington State and Oregon.

Pier 39, San Francisco, California, USA, 4 October 2000. With plenty of free time on their hands, choristers enjoyed sight-seeing trips along the Columbian River in Washington and Mount Saint Helens, the volcano which erupted twenty years earlier.

Golden Gate Bridge, San Francisco, California, USA, 4 October 2000. Only as members of a world-famous choir like Treorchy can this group of singers travel so extensively and enjoy so many wonderful opportunities. It is not just a choir, but a way of life. Long may this continue.